92
VIDOCQ

Edwards, Samuel

The Vidocq Dossier

DATE			

247784

The Vidocq Dossier

François Eugène Vidocq
1775–1857

(Photo. Bibl. nat. Paris)

The Vidocq Dossier

THE STORY OF THE WORLD'S
FIRST DETECTIVE

by Samuel Edwards

HOUGHTON MIFFLIN COMPANY BOSTON   1977

Library of Congress Cataloging in Publication Data
Gerson, Noel Bertram, date
   The Vidocq Dossier: The Story of the World's First Detective
   Bibliography: p.
   1. Vidocq, Eugène François, 1775–1857.   2. Detectives
—France—Biography.
HV7911.V5G47   363.2'092'4 [B]   76-53777
ISBN 0-395-25176-1

Printed in the United States of America

V 10 9 8 7 6 5 4 3 2 1

FOR MARION LILLIAN

If the world will be gulled, let it be gulled.
Robert Burton, *Anatomy of Melancholy*

The Vidocq Dossier

I

A Prelude

LIFE UNDER THE RESTORED BOURBONS was difficult, demanding and dull, and the people of Paris, deprived for more than a decade of the brioche and theaters the Emperor Napoleon had thoughtfully provided, had to find their own entertainment. So the morning of October 17, 1825, was like any other, and a large crowd loitered outside the Royal Court of Municipal Justice on the rue de J. César, a stone's throw from the gutted Bastille. The daily parade of thieves, swindlers and murderers was under way, each of the criminals in chains and accompanied by uniformed policemen wearing the white cockade and sash of King Charles X.

A small, black carriage pulled up at the entrance, and few in the crowd paid much attention to the single occupant who emerged. He was short, no taller than five feet six and one-quarter inches, but he had exceptionally broad shoulders, a thick torso and a massive head. His attire was theatrical and consisted of a square, broad-brimmed hat, a long cape of black broadcloth lined in crimson silk and a pair of polished boots, calf-high, into which he had tucked his trousers. Unlike most of the lawyers, middle-class witnesses and gentlemen who came to the Municipal Court, he carried neither a small sword nor a pistol.

Someone recognized him and murmured his name: "Vidocq."

The crowd surged forward, hoping to get a closer look at

the most infamous citizen of Paris, the man feared and despised by the underworld.

François Eugène Vidocq paused for a moment as he mounted the stone stairs and turned and flung back his cape in an actor's gesture before he disappeared inside the building.

Uniformed gendarmes and soldiers who lined the corridors stiffened to attention and saluted as he passed them, and when he entered the crowded courtroom of President Magistrate Jules Bressie, there was a stir, many in the throng standing and peering at him. He pretended to be unaware of the attention he was drawing and, removing his hat as he sat down in the rear, revealed a thick head of chestnut hair. Some who knew him were surprised, thinking his hair was gray, black or blond and all of them were right. The color of Vidocq's hair changed daily, depending on the disguise he adopted. Today he was being himself.

Everyone in the courtroom knew the basic facts of Vidocq's life, but there were so many stories about him, the majority of which were wildly exaggerated, that no one was aware of the truth. That suited Vidocq's purposes, and only a few of his intimates, among them his mother and his official mistress, realized that he himself was responsible for the many contradictory rumors that made him a man of mystery.

The fundamentals were no secret. He was fifty years old, the son of an Arras baker, and had served with distinction in the army of France under the banners of Louis XVI and the Republic. A love of ladies and adventure and a search for advancement beyond his station had caused him to perpetrate a series of misdemeanors for which he had been imprisoned, but no jail had been able to hold him, and he had escaped repeatedly. Suddenly, in 1809, when he was thirty-four years of age, he won the confidence of the authorities under circumstances never explained, and soon thereafter founded the Brigade de la Sûreté, or security police, the world's first detective bureau devoted exclusively to the solution of crimes. One of the few officials to see continuing service under Napoleon, Louis XVIII, Charles X, and Louis Philippe, he had been responsible for the arrest of many thousands of robbers, burglars, swindlers, highwaymen, confidence men, murderers and other "enemies of France."

It was believed that there were hundreds under his command in what the London newspapers called the Bureau of Detection and Detectives, but no one other than the King and the Minister of the Interior knew for certain how many men and women were in his employ. But his achievements spoke for themselves, and the police of other nations, from England to imperial Russia, to the distant United States of America, were trying to learn his system and techniques so that they could establish their own Bureaus of Detection and Detectives.

The arrival of President Magistrate Bressie and his two associates in the courtroom temporarily drew attention from Vidocq, and the trial of one Lambert on charges of forgery was opened. The prosecutor announced his intention of proving that Lambert, allegedly the possessor of a long criminal record, had tried to cheat a widow and widower, respectively, of their life savings. The defense counsel declared he would prove that Lambert was a respectable citizen, the victim of mistaken identity, who was totally innocent.

The prosecutor requested the right to call M. Vidocq as his first witness, and apologized to the court for the irregularity. Ordinarily the widow and widower who had been Lambert's intended victims would have been called first, but as the court knew, the time of M. Vidocq was valuable, and criminals would make life miserable for honest citizens while he was absent from his post of duty. The defense attorney protested against the suggested irregularity, but was overruled. The Chief of the Sûreté was called to the stand.

Vidocq threw off his cape and was a resplendent figure in a suit of black English woolen, a ruffled shirt of white silk and diamond studs. As he sauntered to the witness box he greeted acquaintances by waving a pair of white calfskin gloves, and he found time to flirt with an attractive young woman before bowing to the President Magistrate, an old friend.

He was soft-spoken and genteel as he began to testify. He had been called into the case because the widow's daughter had been suspicious of Lambert's approach: a letter had been produced, allegedly written by the lady's late husband, claiming that Lambert had been his partner and was entitled to inherit half of his estate.

Vidocq said he had recognized Lambert from his description and his tactics.

The defense counsel objected. Surely the Chief of the Sûreté did not rely on his memory alone in criminal cases.

A smiling Vidocq reached into an inner pocket and drew out a card, one of 60,000 on file at the Sûreté. It gave Lambert's description, criminal record and techniques. It explained his system, telling in detail how he functioned. Vidocq, still soft-spoken, said that although he himself was blessed with a phenomenal memory, he had established his elaborate file system to aid his subordinates.

Lambert's attorney was incredulous. Never before, in France or in any other country, had the police maintained records that told a criminal's entire past.

Vidocq was just warming to his theme, and as he continued, his voice became louder, more compelling. Newspaper reporters, whom he had notified in advance that he would testify, wrote that no star of the Paris stage more completely captured the undivided attention of an audience.

The handwriting on the letter purportedly written by the widow's late husband was actually that of Lambert, Vidocq said, and produced a previous communication written by Lambert to prove his point. With great care he showed the court that flourishes, curlicues and shadings were identical.

Again the defense attorney objected.

Vidocq's voice continued to rise as he explained that he

was utilizing a new science, that of handwriting identification. This new technique had been supported by four distinguished professors from the University of Paris who agreed with his thesis that no two persons had identical handwriting.

The court admitted the document submitted by the Chief of the Sûreté.

With one eye on the reporters, who were taking down every word, Vidocq apologized to the President Magistrate. Soon, he hoped, he would perfect an even more foolproof system: he was convinced, based on the research of others and his own observations, that every individual had unique indentations on the tips of his fingers. These fingerprints, if they were clear, could be enlarged sufficiently to be seen and classified, and might provide a perfect means of identification.

The very idea was far-fetched, but Vidocq was responsible for many inventions, innovations and new ideas that were proving their worth, and as a direct consequence of which thousands of criminals who otherwise would have gone free were being sent to prison every year. The man was a terror, infallible and devastating, who understood the minds of the killer, the robber, the sneak thief and the confidence man better than they understood themselves. It was this knowledge, more than his new methods of crime detection, that made him invincible. He seemed to know, even before a criminal acted, what the man would do.

The defense attorney felt compelled to try again. The document produced by the Chief of the Sûreté for the purpose of handwriting comparison had been altered, he declared, to make it similar to the handwriting of his client.

Vidocq's manner changed again, and he became genial. What the learned counsel had just suggested, he said, was clever, but no such alterations could have been made. With the permission of the court he would demonstrate.

First, the paper on which the communication had been

written was a very special paper. After something was written on it, no changes or alterations of any kind could be made. It was a type of paper as unique as the invention of papyrus. It was perfect for the writing of contracts, wills and other documents intended to last over a period of years. Ultimately the French government would utilize it for the printing of money.

The patents on the paper, which had been developed with the assistance of several chemists, were owned by none other than Vidocq himself. Again looking at the reporters to make certain they didn't miss his next point, he emphasized that he was willing to sell quantities of the special paper to qualified citizens.

Next, Vidocq declared, his attitude becoming firmer, Lambert had fallen into a Sûreté trap, and had written his communication with a special ink surreptitiously supplied by Vidocq himself. The Chief of the Bureau took a small bottle from his pocket and asked permission to demonstrate. The right was granted.

For hundreds of years man had tried to develop a truly indelible ink, one that could not be erased, smudged, changed or washed away. Monks who had worked as scribes in monasteries during the Middle Ages had devoted their entire lives to this goal. Now, at last, such an ink had been developed with the assistance of some highly competent chemists. The patents were owned by Vidocq. The ink, like the special paper, could be purchased by responsible citizens who wanted to protect documents of value.

Handwriting analysis, an indexed criminal record, special paper and special ink combined to overwhelm Lambert. The case came to an abrupt conclusion when the defendant suddenly stood up, admitted he had forged the letter supposedly written by the widow's husband and threw himself on the mercy of the court.

A signal from Vidocq caused the President Magistrate to delay sentencing for an hour.

During this interval the Chief of the Sûreté, displaying his usual compassion for criminals, took the guilty man to a restaurant next door to the Municipal Court. There, after buying Lambert a roasted chicken, some raspberry tarts and a bottle of splendid wine, he suggested there might be a way for the forger to win a much reduced sentence.

The jails were filled with prisoners plotting escapes and planning new criminal exploits. If Lambert listened to his peers, he might have information of value to pass along in strict confidence to a Sûreté representative, in disguise, who would visit him in secret at regular intervals. No other prisoner would know of his affiliation, so the forger would have no need to fear possible reprisals. Others who had cooperated in this manner with the Chief of the Sûreté were living in Paris again as free men or were enjoying the clean air of the countryside, as they preferred.

Lambert knew he could receive a sentence of twenty years and might even be confined in the dreaded "galleys." It was rumored that Vidocq, in his youth, had achieved the impossible feat of escaping from the galleys on at least four separate occasions; most convicts sent to these institutions, however, died within a few years.

Did M. Vidocq happen to know whether the President Magistrate was partial to galley sentencing?

M. Vodocq shrugged, but admitted he might have some slight influence with the judge. As it happened, the Sûreté was eager to place some informants in the prison called the Conciergerie, right here in Paris.

Lambert shuddered. The dregs of the underworld were sent to the old penitentiary, and these hardened thugs, pimps and robbers were not fit companions for a forger, the elite of criminals.

M. Vidocq's second shrug was more eloquent than his first. Lambert accepted the proposal unconditionally. Lambert, after his conviction, would become a police spy.

His benefactor promised nothing, but said he would do

what he could. He intimated that the cooperation of the prisoner in the years ahead would be an essential element of the bargain.

The Chief of the Sûreté was admitted to the private chambers of President Magistrate Bressie, and a few words were exchanged by the pair who had learned over the years to admire and respect each other. It was not accidental that Vidocq had established similar working relations with most members of the Paris bench. Before taking his leave it is possible he did the President Magistrate some small favor, perhaps giving him the address of a pretty actress he admired, or loaning him money, without collateral, at rates lower than those the moneylenders of Paris were charging. It was common knowledge that the Chief of the Sûreté was well acquainted — others used stronger terms — with every attractive, available young woman in the city. Fewer people knew about his reputed moneylending, and although he never admitted such activities, he did not deny them either.

His business at the Municipal Court concluded after a profitable stay of only two hours and Vidocq returned to his waiting carriage, again accepting the admiration of the crowds. Perhaps he had a typically busy morning ahead of him: a visit to the Louvre, where he might return some indiscreet love letters written by a member of the royal family, and which, in some never-explained manner, had been retrieved by the resourceful detective; a meeting with his principal aides to discuss the measures they would take that night to catch the members of a gang intending to rob a warehouse; a budget meeting with the Minister of the Interior, who insisted in vain that the Sûreté ledgers be opened for his inspection; and finally, before donning one of his innumerable disguises and lying in wait for the robbers, possibly a brief interlude with a modiste he fancied. The only question in Vidocq's mind might have been whether to postpone the liaison with the modiste until later in the evening. In that way he could dine with her at his leisure after rounding up the warehouse robbers.

On second thought, perhaps he would finish work in time to drop in at one of the theaters and arrange a dinner engagement with one of the many actresses who clamored for his attentions. Before the day ended, too, he wanted to find a spare hour in which to examine a painting he was thinking of adding to his private gallery, and perhaps buy a handsome silver coffee service for his collection. It had come to his attention that a prominent gentleman who was financially embarrassed was eager to dispose of various belongings in order to avoid bankruptcy, and the prudent detective wanted to strike a bargain or two with him before the news became public and the prices of paintings and silver rose.

It was not true that Vidocq collected works of art and objects of precious metals — any one of which cost him more than his annual wages of 5000 francs — because he was vain and was trying to copy the opulent living style of the aristocracy. His enemies delighted in denigrating him by telling such stories, but they were mistaken, as usual. Good paintings, solid gold and sterling silver appreciated over the years and were worth more than cash in a vault. At fifty Vidocq had a long life ahead, having sworn he would live to the age of one hundred, and he wanted security so that he could concentrate on other things. Already unique and renowned, his mind seethed with new projects, new inventions, new ways to achieve even greater, lasting fame.

The major problem involved in the study of Vidocq's life a century and a half after his own time is the separation of fact from legend. This difficulty is caused in part by his own secretiveness, which was basic to his nature, and which was combined with a tendency to romanticize his genuine achievements and his exploits.

Even more important, however, was his close association

with a number of the leading French literary men of the nineteenth century, all of whom — with Vidocq's pleased connivance — took full advantage of their friendship with him to borrow freely from his life, career and ideas for their own work. Often it proves impossible to determine what was real and what was enlarged or changed in some way.

Someone other than Vidocq actually wrote his best-selling autobiography. Other books about him, supposedly authorized by him, were written anonymously, as were magazine articles and interviews. His exploits captured the imagination of French men of letters, who were intrigued by his personality and wrote about him freely.

No substantial manuscripts written in his own hand have ever been found. His memoranda on scientific methods of crime detection, which were curt and precise, were dictated to subordinates in the Sûreté. It must be therefore assumed that his autobiography and a number of other books about him were penned by admiring friends. The originals of these manuscripts conveniently vanished during Vidocq's own lifetime, so it may be that he disposed of them himself.

Careful in his investigative reports to present only facts that could be demonstrated, Vidocq was happy to allow his friends to write about him and his exploits as they pleased, provided that they praised him, which they invariably did. So some phases of his life defy the biographer in search of accurate details.

Balzac was one of Vidocq's intimates and on occasion, when spending an evening together, they tried to outdo each other in the telling of tall tales. Balzac's stories, based on his observations and knowledge of human nature, were candidly fanciful and told for the entertainment of his guests. Vidocq, always the hero of his own accounts, supposedly drew on his own experiences and told stories he swore were factual. From time to time he proved he was telling the literal truth, and Balzac was overwhelmed.

Never one to waste a character, Balzac used Vidocq as the prototype for his Inspector Vautrin, who appeared in a number of the *Comédie humaine* novels. When borrowing from real life most novelists try to conceal that fact, and Balzac usually took care to disguise his characters. It was unnecessary to take such precautions in dealing with his Inspector, however, and newspaper advertisements for his books openly boasted that the publicity-hungry Vidocq appeared in their pages.

Another titan close to Vidocq was Victor Hugo, who dined with him frequently in the restaurants both men favored in the vicinity of the Palais Royal. Hugo ate and drank prodigiously, while the detective confined himself to a simple dish or two and never consumed more than a single glass of wine at a sitting, but Hugo wrote that his friend's stories so fascinated him that he sometimes forgot to eat or drink.

The extent to which Hugo may have been responsible for works attributed to Vidocq cannot be ascertained. When Vidocq visited London at the age of seventy and was asked directly by a newspaper interviewer whether Hugo had written any of his books or articles, the founder of the Brigade of the Sûreté was willing to admit only that the great author had "advised" him and had "criticized" his style.

All that can be said with certainty is that Vidocq and Hugo had one trait in common. Both were irresistibly drawn to actresses and modistes — most of them also part-time courtesans — willing to grant favors to men of stature and means, and they exchanged mistresses at least twice.

Alexandre Dumas the elder, another of the great authors who counted Vidocq among his close friends, had an insatiable appetite for women and wine, and, by his own admission, was saved from embarrassment on several occasions by the noted detective. One morning Dumas awakened to discover that his wallet had been emptied and a quantity of valuable silver had been taken by a women with whom he had spent the night. Unfortunately he couldn't remember her name, and at dinner that day he confessed to several friends that he had been fleeced.

Vidocq, the first police official to have systematically established a vast network of informants in the underworld, quietly went to work on the author's behalf. Less than twenty-four hours later Dumas's silver was recovered, as were the contents of his wallet, minus a sum that enabled the woman to beat a discreet retreat from Paris for a time.

The author of hundreds of books, Dumas used the experiences of everyone he knew as grist for his mill, and Vidocq was no exception. On the contrary, the founder of the Sûreté supplied his friend with scores of stories that found their way into print as incidents in Dumas's novels. A readily identifiable Vidocq appeared in these tales, and invariably triumphed over the forces of evil.

Eugène Sue, one of the more earnest of nineteenth-century social reformers, owed a more serious debt to Vidocq and made no secret of it. His belief, expressed in a number of his novels, that the basic causes of crime were poverty and privation in childhood grew out of principles that Vidocq frequently elaborated. Sue also became an ardent advocate of Vidocq's view that the hardened criminal could be rehabilitated if given an opportunity to earn an honest living and gain self-respect. Vidocq spent a fortune in an attempt to prove his theory, and Sue became its publicist.

It is unlikely that Sue wrote any of the books, articles or treatises that appeared under Vidocq's name as they were notably lacking in the smooth elegance of style that marked Sue's own work. It is possible, however, that the writing of pieces on the background of crime and criminals and, above all, the articles on how to transform a scoundrel into a good citizen were edited by Sue. Certainly he maintained a lively interest in everything Vidocq did.

One of the detective's most vocal champions was another of his frequent dinner companions, Théophile Gautier, the most influential literary critic of the era. Gautier loved delicate prose, delicate imagery and delicate women, not necessarily in that order, and, himself sedentary, was impressed by men of action. In Vidocq he found someone who calculated every move in advance, then acted accordingly, and he was proud to be known as the good friend of the Sûreté's founder.

Two or three minor writers of the period who wrote extensively about Vidocq — one of them may have been the actual author of his autobiography — were protégés of Gautier. So the critic may have been influential in enhancing the detective's renown without making direct literary contributions himself.

Vidocq's relations with Alphonse de Lamartine were complex. The first of the renowned nineteenth-century Romantic poets in France, Lamartine, after a career as a soldier and diplomat, became actively interested in politics during the Revolution of 1830, when he was forty years old. Elected to the Chamber of Deputies in 1833, he served there for the next eighteen years, and for a time during the Revolution of 1848 he was the head of the provisional Republic until he was defeated for the presidency by Louis Napoleon.

If Vidocq and Lamartine were somewhat less than intimate, they nevertheless saw each other regularly, dined together occasionally and met at the homes of others. Vidocq's admiration for Lamartine was genuine, as it was for all men of letters. But the poet-politician was wary in his dealings with the detective. Vidocq, like so many policemen, had little interest in politics and didn't care whether he served royalists or republicans. He courted politicians only to hold his job: catching criminals and making France safe for honest citizens. His refusal to join one or another faction during a half-century of upheaval made him enemies in high places.

Lamartine, ambitious almost to the end of his own days, wanted to offend no one who might be helpful to him. So he took care not to become too close to Vidocq, of whom the uniformed police were violently jealous, after he left the Sûreté to found the world's first private detective bureau. According to a story that many contemporaries believed, Lamartine refused to call on Vidocq in 1857, when he was dying, for fear of harming his own image.

In any event, so many authors of note wrote about Vidocq under their own names, under pseudonyms and under his name that many of the true facts of his life are buried in exaggerations, colorful myths and outright lies. Some truths have never been unearthed. This book is an attempt to set the record straight.

II

PARISIANS AND FOREIGNERS passing through the Pas-de-Calais Department in northern France during the 1770's almost always stayed overnight in Arras because it boasted the only first-rate inns in the area. But these visitors, if they thought of it at all, undoubtedly regarded it as a quiet market town, its most notable feature being its superb medieval architecture. Its once-thriving tapestry industry was in the doldrums, and life on the surface was dull.

Appearances were deceptive, however, and outsiders had no way of knowing that the people of Arras were endowed with an intellectual curiosity and a ruggedly independent spirit that made them unique. It was not accidental that a son of the Robespierre family should become the most fanatical radical leader of the French Revolution, or that a son of the Vidocq family should found a new profession based on scientific principles, that of the detective. The reform-seeking priests of Arras, regarded by many of their contemporaries as radicals, were largely responsible for the ferment. The clergy thought of Paris as depraved, an opinion that was bolstered by the scandalous conduct of the guests who stopped at the town's inns. The sons of Arras were taught the benefits of sobriety and hard work.

Nicholas-François-Joseph Vidocq was a baker whose skill and industry had made him the best in Arras, so he was a person of consequence in the community. He lived with his pretty wife, Henriette-Françoise-Josèphe, on the upper floors of a solid, thirteenth-century house, maintaining his bakery and shop on the ground floor. He was famous for his secret recipe for bread, which he had inherited from his own father and then improved, and most of what he baked was sold to the leading inns of the district.

Regular customers bought the rest, their names checked against a list, and it was impossible for strangers to purchase even a single loaf. Nicholas Vidocq could have doubled his business had he wanted to expand, but he was content with the comfortable living he earned, and was too conservative to take unnecessary financial risks. He was treated with respect when he went to church on Sunday mornings, his wife on his arm, and he had no desire to broaden his horizons.

The couple's first child, a son, was born on July 24, 1775, and was christened François Eugène. His father took it for granted that he would grow up to take his place in the bakery. His mother, more ambitious, wanted him to obtain the best of all possible educations and even dared to hope he might become a priest.

The child entered the local school of the Franciscan Fathers at the age of five, two years earlier than his peers, and twelve months later he could read, write and do sums. It was obvious from the outset that he was exceptionally bright, and the Franciscans pushed him to the limits of his capacity. By the time he was nine he was learning Greek, Latin, chemistry, astronomy and rhetoric. He could memorize long passages from plays and philosophical works without effort, mastered principles of physics with seeming ease and read avidly about the New World, often expressing the intention of going to America and making his fortune there.

In spite of his aptitudes, however, young Vidocq won no prizes in scholarship. Books could provide him with only a fraction of what he wanted to learn, and neither the classroom nor the bakery could confine him. Frequently he sneaked off to the more expensive inns, where he ran errands for wealthy guests, and it was difficult for his father to scold him when he came home with a full purse.

At the age of nine or ten he happened to walk past a hall where young gentlemen were fencing, and he developed a new passion. Master swordsmen were amused by his interest and taught him the art, also instructing him in the use of the pistol. By the time the baker's son was twelve he was as accomplished with sword and pistol as any blueblood twice his age.

Around this same time he also developed another avocation that he would follow for the rest of his days. He discovered girls, and from the start Vidocq's taste was impeccable. Only the truly beautiful girls interested him, and he was bored by the ordinary ones. Even at an early age he demanded challenges from his relationships.

By the time young Vidocq entered his teens no one could influence him, as his parents and the Franciscans were discovering. A company of actors came to Arras for a few days, and when they left town the boy disappeared. The authorities searched the district for him in vain, and three weeks passed before he was found, less than thirty miles from home. He had joined the players, and whenever members of the constabulary appeared, he immediately disguised himself as a feminine member of the troupe, even playing small girls' roles on several occasions.

No one, least of all Vidocq himself, realized that he had already found his true vocation. He had a genius for disguise, and could change his voice and manner as easily as he could change clothes.

On one occasion, when his name had become a byword, he was asked by his friend and admirer Honoré de Balzac to explain his talents. Vidocq replied that the change in one's appearance came from within, and was a science rather than an art. He observed the way an old man walked, the way a young woman gestured, the way a peasant chewed a blade of grass or a gallant took a pinch of snuff. "Observe what you would become, then act accordingly," he told Balzac, "and you will be transformed."

Soon after Vidocq was forcibly returned to the home of his parents he got into trouble again, this time for bedding the daughter of an English viscount who had stopped overnight with his family at an Arras inn. When it developed that the girl was seventeen and he was only thirteen, the local magistrate refused to punish the boy, and the whole town was amused.

In spite of his continuing escapades Vidocq was thinking seriously about his future, which included neither Arras nor a life as a baker. He had seen the way the wealthy dressed and ate when they engaged their suites at the local inns, he had watched them drive off in their huge carriages and he had stared in wonder at their gold swords, their gems and their beautiful ladies. Not even the outbreak of the French Revolution in 1789, when he was fourteen, could dim his ardor for the life he wanted. He would become a prosperous gentleman, and the servants at the inns would bow low before him.

Opportunities in France were limited, so the precocious Vidocq decided he would migrate to America, where he hoped to make a fortune. He confided in a young actress who happened to be playing in Arras, and she encouraged him. They would elope together and would board a ship bound for Philadelphia at Calais.

The fourteen-year-old boy took the money he had been saving since early childhood and went off with the young woman to Calais. There, he awakened one morning to find that the actress had vanished, taking all of his money and most of his clothes. He had to work his way home and vowed that never again would he allow a woman to fool him.

Vidocq took to swordplay with a vengeance, neglecting his studies in order to practice fencing and, by the time he was fifteen, he had earned the grudging respect of many adults. By now he had filled out, his torso was thick and he had great strength in his arms; in spite of his short stature, no sensible man wanted to cross swords in anger with him.

Again the attraction of a pretty face caused him problems, and this time they were grave. He and a fencing master quarreled over a young woman and Vidocq killed the man in a duel. He was placed under arrest, and escaped imprisonment only because the court allowed him to join the army. He promptly enlisted and was assigned to the elite Bourbon Regiment. Like other recruits he was given no training worthy of the name and was sent off to the Low Countries where he was certain to see action within a very short time.

The French need for men in uniform was desperate. King Louis and his Austrian wife, Queen Marie Antoinette, were virtual prisoners at Versailles; the crown had been stripped of its powers, and the nation's sentiment in favor of the establishment of a republic was soaring. These harsh developments alarmed Europe's other monarchs, and the Hapsburgs of Austria and Spain had formed a loose alliance with Great Britain and a number of the German principalities. Imperial Russia was prepared to act, too, and for all practical purposes France was at war with all of her neighbors. Her only ally was the infant United States, whom she had aided in the American struggle for independence, and whose people admired her increasingly republican sentiments. But the new nation was weak, far away and incapable of making any significant contribution to the French cause.

Vidocq's military career, which was sporadic, lasted for approximately five years, and the better part of it is documented by records still in existence. He took part in the battle of Mons, where he fought with distinction. At Valmy he refused to retreat when the enemy advanced, rallied his entire company and was promoted on the spot to corporal.

Discovering that officers received much higher pay than

enlisted men, enjoyed many privileges and were given superior billets, Vidocq deserted from the Bourbon Regiment and
joined the 11th Chasseurs as a junior lieutenant. At the battle
of Jemappes he led his platoon into combat and proved
himself an able commander, so he was promoted to senior
lieutenant.

Various indiscretions including duels, the accumulation of
staggering gambling debts and a foolhardy love affair with
the wife of his colonel made it necessary once again for Vidocq to leave. His supposed adventures during this underground period, as they appear in his autobiography, are so
bizarre that they must be dismissed as nonsense. The author
of this work, whoever he may have been, became the victim
of his own imagination, and the supposed events that took
place read like an inferior eighteenth-century adventure
novel.

Ultimately Vidocq reappeared under another name, having
adopted the uniform and identity of a captain. His military
exploits, which have been authenticated by records that still
exist, were very real, indeed, and he fought with such valor
on the Dutch front that he received a personal commendation
from the French commanding general.

When Vidocq wasn't fighting he was causing more trouble
for himself, but it is difficult to draw a clear picture of his
activities during these active years. Suffice it to say that he
learned self-reliance even though he indulged his whims and
rarely exercised self-discipline. At this stage in his development he was a hedonist who found most of his pleasure in
excitement for its own sake. Material comforts appear to have
meant relatively little to him.

Certainly Vidocq was a superb swordsman, and it is a matter of record that he won eleven duels during his army career, in each of them satisfying his honor but avoiding trouble with the law by trying to inflict minor flesh wounds on
his opponents. But the claim made in his autobiography that
he fought fifteen duels during his first half-year in the army is

absurd. According to this account he won all of these sword fights, killing six men and severely wounding five others. As a soldier he lived under martial law and would have been executed had he engaged in such indiscriminate killing of comrades in arms.

There can be little doubt, however, that he was an untamed spirit during his youth, that he was willing to fight for any cause in which he believed. He happened to come home to Arras on sick leave in 1794, after Louis XVI and Marie Antoinette had been executed, and France, under the reign of the Terror, was in a state of near anarchy.

He still felt a deep affection for the Franciscan Fathers who had educated him, and one day, when he saw a gang of republican bullies trying to break into their property, he routed them with his sword and pistol. A few days later he created greater problems for himself when he berated three cavalrymen who were assisting the public executioner as several noblewomen were led to the guillotine. He was arrested for obstructing justice, and it seemed likely that he himself would face the guillotine.

A young woman whom he had known slightly since childhood saw the incident in the square in front of the Hôtel de Ville, however, and intervened on his behalf. Louise Chevalier, a year younger than Vidocq, had been in love with him for a long time, which was fortunate, as her father, Henri Chevalier, was the chairman of the Terror in Arras, and the young soldier was pardoned. He rejoined his regiment without delay.

A scant three months later he returned to Arras to recuperate after being wounded in battle, and as soon as he arrived, Louise informed him she was pregnant. A marriage was arranged in haste, the young bridegroom being given no voice in the matter. His father-in-law saw to it that he was mustered out of the army, and his father bought him a greengrocer's store so that he could support himself and his wife.

His unhappiness was compounded when he learned that

Louise had tricked him into marriage, inventing the story that she was expecting a baby. The couple quarreled so violently that Henri Chevalier was afraid his daughter would suffer bodily harm and had his son-in-law sent off to the army again.

On Vidocq's next leave, early in 1795, he returned to Arras without sending advance word, and found his wife in bed with an officer of the 17th Chasseurs. The frightened Louise managed to summon the constables before the enraged Vidocq could kill her lover. Chevalier, embarrassed by his daughter's indiscretion, was glad to see his angry son-in-law mount his horse and canter out of town.

At no time had Vidocq been in love with his wife, but her infidelity was a blow to his pride, and instead of returning to the army he decided the time had come, once again, to try making his fortune. He went to Brussels, where criminals long had been preying on nobles and wealthy merchants who had fled from France. There he called himself Captain Rousseau and, setting up housekeeping with a young actress known to posterity only as Emilie, he joined a band of card sharks. He had learned to become adept at handling playing cards in the army and suffered no pangs of conscience as he cheated honest men at nightly games.

After a few months of precarious high living he was picked up by the authorities, who believed that Captain Rousseau was an army deserter. Preferring to hand him over to military justice rather than try him in a civilian court, they sent him off under heavy guard to the garrison at Lille.

Vidocq knew that the French army would not be interested in his brief career as a card shark, but his pose as a captain of dragoons was far more serious. He would be revealed as an impostor and a deserter from his own regiment and could face years in prison.

That night, when his escort camped in a field, he demonstrated the agility for which he would become famous. Breaking free of his bonds, he managed to escape undetected from his guards. Doubling back to Brussels because he rightly believed no one would think of searching for him there, Vidocq celebrated his twentieth birthday by becoming a fugitive from justice.

III

VIDOCQ KNEW when he returned to Brussels that he couldn't
afford another brush with the constabulary, so he renewed an
acquaintance with a wealthy, attractive widow, many years
his senior, who had flirted with him previously. Soon he
moved in with her and lived with her for some weeks, but
the idyll turned sour when she wanted to marry him. He felt
compelled to tell her the truth about his situation, and they
parted, the grateful lady giving him the enormous sum of
1500 gold francs, far more than his father earned in a year.

He went off to Paris, seeing the city for the first time and
falling in love with it. He took a suite at an expensive inn,
became involved with an equally expensive courtesan and
soon was parted from his money. Paris was no place for pau-
pers, so he drifted north to Lille where he had an affair with
a woman identified in his autobiography only as Francine.
She had another lover, a captain of engineers, and when Vidocq found them dining together he made a violent, jealous
scene that caused him to be arrested. He was sentenced to
his first prison term, and was sent to the local jail for three
months.

In jail an incident occurred that would influence his entire
life: he and two others felt sorry for a peasant who was serving six years for stealing grain to feed his starving family; and
a week later, miraculously, the warden received a formal pardon that set the peasant free. Twenty-four hours later it was

discovered that the pardon was a forgery, and Vidocq, who was guilty, was implicated. He was ordered to stand a new trial at the end of his term, but he knew what would happen, and with the aid of the repentant Francine, he escaped. He was captured, but escaped a second time.

He went in disguise to Ostend, where he worked for a short time with a band of smugglers, but was arrested because he lacked identity papers. Francine, who had accompanied him, helped him to get away yet again, and he joined a troupe of traveling players, one of whom betrayed him. He made repeated attempts to escape, some of them successful, but each time he was recaptured and ultimately he was brought to trial for the forgery of the pardon. Whether the authorities also realized that he was a deserter is not known.

The evidence against him was overwhelming, and Vidocq was sentenced to serve eight years in the "galleys," special prisons for hardened criminals who were required to wear leg and arm chains at all times and to don leaded boots whenever they left their cells. These places were not necessarily actual galleys; the name was generic, and was applied to all maximum-security penitentiaries.

Vidocq was sent first to the maximum-security prison of Bicêtre, on the outskirts of Paris, and after several blundering attempts to escape he was finally transferred, late in 1798, to the galleys in Brest, where convicts were employed as slave laborers in the navy's shipyards. He was twenty-two years old, and would be a broken man of thirty by the time he was released.

Few prisons anywhere were more brutal, and the living conditions were shocking. Prisoners were never free of their chains; as many as 600 slept in a single barracks hall on hard benches; they were fed slops; worked at hard labor for sixteen hours per day, seven days per week; and were beaten when they either balked or were no longer capable of performing. Vidocq thought only in terms of escape, knowing he could not survive such treatment for eight years.

Displaying remarkable agility, he accomplished the almost impossible: he acquired a sailor's uniform, which he managed to hide, stole a file and cut through his chains. He was free for the better part of a year and even dared to visit Arras where he learned that his father had died. He also discovered that his wife was pregnant by another man.

Vidocq, who knew nothing about the sea, signed on as a crew member of a privateer that preyed on English merchant shipping in the Channel and the North Sea. A number of prizes were taken, and Vidocq sent his share of the profits to his mother.

In the summer of 1799 he was arrested because he lacked proper identity papers and was recognized. His sentence was automatically doubled, and he was sent to the galleys at Toulon. There, he was permanently confined to the hulk of an old ship-of-the-line with other prisoners who were regarded as so dangerous that they were not sent ashore to work. His fellow prisoners were murderers, rapists and men who had committed mayhem. Living conditions were even worse than they had been in Brest, and the jailers closed their eyes when a convict died in a fight.

Vidocq had hidden a considerable sum of money on his person, and experience taught him how to spend it. First he paid a guard to give him chains that were actually screwed together, although they appeared to be riveted. Then, little by little, he acquired a wardrobe that consisted of two outfits, one a sailor's uniform and the other a gentleman's suit, shirt and boots. He was determined not to rot on the hulk for sixteen years, even though he knew that if he should be captured again he would be beaten so severely that he might well be crippled for the rest of his life.

Vidocq waited until a navy frigate docked nearby and the sailors were given shore leave. The guard on the hulk was changed at sundown, and, for a period of a minute or two, the convicts were left untended. Vidocq, who was already wearing the sailor's uniform under his prison rags, used those moments to slip away and mingling with the sailors on shore, he managed to leave the naval base.

By the time his escape was discovered and the alarm given, he was safe for the night in the bed of a prostitute. The next morning he dressed in his gentleman's attire, but found that now he faced a new problem: that of leaving town without the identity papers required of everyone departing from France's most important naval base. Again Vidocq's ingenuity came to his rescue, and he joined a funeral procession walking behind a carriage-drawn coffin to a cemetery beyond the city gates. The mourners were not required to show their papers, and once again he was free.

Unable to earn an honest living in a small town for fear his identity would be discovered, Vidocq slowly made his way northward with the aid of the criminal underground. As one who had twice escaped from the galleys, he had a real stature in the world of murderers and thieves. His goal was Paris where he hoped to find anonymity.

An obliging band of highwaymen gave him a horse and an escort as he traveled through Provence, but he ran into difficulties when he reached Lyons. Two former convicts whom he knew asked him to join a gang of robbers that was terrorizing the prosperous city, but Vidocq refused, never having committed a violent act for gain. Out of spite the robbers denounced him to the authorities, and he was arrested. He faced a return to the galleys for life.

Jean-Pierre Dubois, the President of the Lyons police, was a shrewd, ambitious administrator who was trying to establish a reputation for himself and win a top position in the Paris police hierarchy by making Lyons the most crime-free city in France. He deserves the credit for hauling François Eugène Vidocq out of the seemingly hopeless morass into which he had fallen and for setting him on the right path.

An investigation of Vidocq's background showed Dubois that the young man was actually guilty of only one misdeed, that of forging a pardon because he had felt sorry for a family man who had been subjected to harsh punishment after committing a minor crime. The soldier of fortune from Arras was precisely the person Dubois needed to further his own ends.

Vidocq was offered a simple proposition: no charges would be placed against him, and he would be given his freedom if he became a police informer. The alternative was so dreadful that Vidocq accepted, and his own career was launched.

He knew enough about the activities of the robbers who had betrayed him to have them arrested, and two members of the gang were convicted of murder. Vidocq then went into the Lyons underworld disguised as a procurer, and his pose was so authentic that he actually persuaded two prostitutes to share their earnings with him and to set up housekeeping with him. The underworld accepted him without question.

Within a short time the Lyons police became busier. A robber who had killed at least three of his victims was apprehended, tried and executed. A family of pickpockets was sent to prison. A band of house thieves was captured, and most of the goods they had stolen were retrieved from a warehouse. Then another murderer was caught, but only Vidocq's testimony could convict him, so the informer moved into the open.

Vidocq's court appearance made it impossible for him to go underground in Lyons again, but the grateful President of the Lyons police, Dubois, kept his word, giving him valid papers that identified him as an itinerant peddler. For the present, at least, he would not be sent to the galleys and hoped he could have his forgery conviction reversed on the grounds that he had acted out of compassion, with no hope of personal gain.

Vidocq went without delay to Paris where he found a position in a large shop on the rue Saint-Martin. He worked there for the better part of the year before the proprietress discharged him for being overly familiar with her female employees.

He went home to Arras, where, thanks to an elaborate disguise that included a mustache, a full beard and dyed hair, only his mother knew him. Posing as a former Austrian prisoner of war, he plunged into an affair with a widow who owned a small drygoods shop. He went to work in the establishment, and within six months the business doubled. At the end of a year someone recognized him, and Vidocq fled to Rouen, taking his mother and mistress with him.

He opened another drygoods store and worked so diligently that after two years it was one of the most prosperous establishments in the city. Ultimately he was recognized again, this time by a former convict, and the dreary flight had to be repeated.

The vicissitudes endured by Vidocq during this unhappy period are repetitious: he went to Versailles, where he established another successful business, and when betrayed there he joined the crew of yet another privateer for the better part of a year. Forced to run again, he rejoined the army and soon was promoted to corporal, then to sergeant. He leaped from the military to civilian life; he fought; he earned money; he took care of his mother and he made love to a succession of remarkably faithful mistresses. Always on the run, living dangerously from year to year, he developed a special knack for averting catastrophe.

There is no hint in his autobiography, no indication in any of the other books written about him that he was even aware of the momentous developments that were changing France and the world. In 1795 an obscure brigadier general, Napoleon Bonaparte, became commander of the Army of the Interior. Two years later he was victorious over Austria in Italy and in 1799 he made himself First Consul, the master of France.

Napoleon drew up a new code of laws and stabilized the chaotic finances of France; he reformed the educational system, transformed the political hierarchy and, while granting religious freedom to people of all faiths, simultaneously mended relations with the Vatican. The French were granted personal liberties unknown anywhere except in the Anglo-

Saxon world, provided Napoleon himself was not criticized. He launched an extensive program of public works, encouraged the arts and expanded France's empire, even while selling such difficult-to-govern possessions as the Louisiana Territory to the United States in 1803.

Crowning himself Emperor in 1804, Napoleon thereafter displayed a military genius unequaled since the exploits of Julius Caesar. Late in 1805 he smashed the armies of Austria and imperial Russia at Austerlitz and eight months later he dissolved the one-thousand-year-old Holy Roman Empire. In 1806 he crushed the Prussians and occupied Berlin. The following year he defeated Russia so decisively that Tsar Alexander was forced to sign a humiliating treaty. In 1808 he invaded Spain and Portugal and in 1809, after his great victory at Wagram, he forced the Austrians to their knees. He placed his brothers and sisters on thrones, creating new kingdoms for them when it suited his political expediency, and in 1809 he divorced his wife, Josephine, a native of Martinique, because she had not given him a son to carry on his line. Although the world didn't yet know it, he was already negotiating for the hand of the Archduchess Marie Louise, sister of the Austrian Emperor.

Under Napoleon Paris became the capital of Europe, the capital of the civilized world. For a thousand years it had retained its French flavor, to be sure, but as a city it was no more impressive than Berlin, Brussels or Madrid. Napoleon gave it new boulevards and monuments. His own soldiers and those of allied nations came to Paris on leaves of absence and were entertained in new taverns, elaborate brothels and amusement parks. Diplomats and princes, bankers and businessmen from a score of countries came to Paris, its population now swollen to more than one million inhabitants, and most of them stayed at new hotels and hostelries, dining at new inns.

For the first time in its history Paris attained the international flavor that has remained one of its more pronounced characteristics down to the present day. Signs appeared on the doors of shops announcing that various foreign languages were spoken, and interpreters were in great demand. Costumes native to other lands were seen on the streets, and no one bothered to gape at them.

Paris was a wartime boom city, and adventurers and thieves, scoundrels and demimondaines from all parts of Europe flocked there. The crime rate soared, although it remained astonishingly low by late twentieth-century standards.

Under a tradition that necessity had forced into being in the Middle Ages, some parts of the city were sanctuaries for thieves, robbers, swindlers and even murderers. Narrow, winding streets, dark alleyways and crowded living quarters had made it difficult for the police to hunt down their quarries, and the sullen opposition to authority displayed by the inhabitants of these quarters made it dangerous for constables to appear there.

The vigorous Henri IV had tried to open these sections of Paris to his police and so had Louis XIV, but both had failed. Those who expected Napoleon to alter conditions didn't understand the nature of his reign. He and his secret police had no interest in common criminals.

Joseph Fouché, Napoleon's extraordinary Minister of Police and the Interior, was rewarded for ten years of remarkably efficient service in 1809 by being made the Duc d'Otrante. His secret police were widespread in France and in the other lands incorporated into the Empire. Opponents of the regime were hunted mercilessly, then cast into prison. The secret police of modern times in Nazi Germany, Soviet Russia and many other nations were modeled on Fouché's organization.

It must be stressed that the new Duc d'Otrante was interested only in traitors and other subversives. His antennae were exclusively political, and the thousands in his employ devoted their efforts to the preservation of the Empire. Let subversives who threatened the Emperor try to hide in the slum sanctuaries and they would be rooted out, then hauled off to prison. But the stability of the throne was in no way disturbed by thieves, so Fouché ignored them. No accurate crime statistics were kept, but Vidocq later estimated that one murder of passion or greed was committed in the city every twenty-four hours. Robberies were commonplace, and men of standing and wealth went out accompanied by armed guards. Even citizens of the growing middle class hired custodians to keep watch over their houses, but the number of burglaries committed each day continued to grow. Blackmail was a common, universal crime, and confidence men and women preyed on the innocent. Figures released by Vidocq in 1826 indicated that there were more than 5000 pickpockets in Paris in 1809. No one bothered to count the prostitutes, but hundreds of them robbed their customers nightly.

Crime flourished, it was said, because Napoleon was too busy conducting the affairs of the greatest empire the modern world had ever seen. And until he took personal notice and gave the word to act, the murderers, robbers and confidence men were safe.

The time was overripe for someone wielding a stiff broom with a strong arm to clean out the Augean stables, and in 1809 Vidocq began to be involved with the world around him. He had continued to move every year or two, and although captured several times, had escaped each time. Now he was living in Paris with his mother and a mysterious mistress named Annette, about whom little is known, with whom he conducted a small but successful drygoods business.

One day, out of the blue, he put Annette in charge of the shop and went to work, secretly, for the Criminal Division of the Paris Prefecture of Police.

Two totally different stories account for this sudden, dramatic move on the part of the thirty-four-year-old fugitive from justice. According to one, he was being blackmailed by some ex-convicts who had recognized him. When they demanded that he join their gang in the commission of robberies that sometimes involved murder, he privately balked and went to the police with the offer of a deal. He would produce the evidence that would send the gang to prison provided the police, in return, would grant him immunity from arrest and the opportunity to petition the courts for a reversal of his forgery sentence, the one real crime he had ever committed.

The second story is more colorful and infinitely more romantic. The divorced Empress Josephine, still regarded by many as the most fascinating woman in France, was living at Malmaison, a small estate outside Paris that she had shared with the Emperor in happier days. Only those who sought no imperial favors came to see her, so she had few visitors, and the sentries assigned to guard her became lax. One morning late in October, 1809, the Duc d'Otrante personally called in the head of the Criminal Division of the Prefecture to announce that an emerald necklace, which Napoleon had given her as a wedding gift, had been stolen. The Emperor was furious and demanded that it be recovered without delay because his enemies would claim he had arranged the theft. This much of the story is known to be true.

The police went to work on the case, but in vain, and no leads were developed. The Criminal Division had no contacts in the underworld, and literally didn't know where to begin their search. At this point, according to the legend, Vidocq appeared, offering to find the necklace in return for immunity and the chance to gain a full pardon.

The offer was accepted, and Vidocq went to work in his own way, spending hours in taverns frequented by fences and going to inns where the elite of the underworld ate. According to the story — which well might be true, as he later performed similar incredible deeds — he went back to the police in less than three days, telling them not only the identity of the thieves, but the place where the necklace was hidden.

It is a matter of record that Josephine's emeralds were recovered. Whether Vidocq was actually responsible for their recovery cannot be proved, but the story goes on to the predictable conclusion that Napoleon, relieved because he had been saved embarrassment, received Vidocq in a private audience and then ordered that he be given a post worthy of his talents.

Whatever the reason for his employment, Vidocq found his true vocation a few weeks after his thirty-fourth birthday. The police hired him as a spy, but he had no intention of spending the rest of his days as an informer, a precarious profession at best. Officialdom's lack of contacts in the Paris underworld made it impossible to curb the rising crime wave, and he was already evolving a plan that would create a secure place for himself on the right side of the law.

IV

THE PREFECTURE OF POLICE gave Vidocq a simple but dangerous assignment: he was sent to La Force prison in Paris as a recaptured convict awaiting a new trial, with a supposed life sentence in the galleys a certainty. It was arranged that he would send twice-weekly reports to the Criminal Division and would use the faithful Annette as his messenger. Each Tuesday and Friday she would dine in a small restaurant near the apartment where she continued to live with Vidocq's mother and there she would be joined by a police courier who would relay the messages Vidocq had given her.

The system was effective. Vidocq was held in high esteem by other prisoners because he had twice escaped from the galleys, and he immediately became a leader of the compound, with others confiding in him and seeking his advice. Considerable quantities of contraband hidden in Paris warehouses were recovered, and, even more important, two murders were solved. None of the prisoners dreamed that their "distinguished" colleague was an informer.

While playing this role Vidocq formed an association with a somewhat younger man named Barthélemy Lacour, who was known as Coco in the underworld. He was a petty thief, pickpocket and pimp, and Vidocq took care to cultivate the friendship. Coco was a man who followed orders and he was already marked for future service in his new mentor's grand design.

For a full year Vidocq remained in prison, serving his new masters faithfully and obtaining important information for them. He grew tired of his confinement, however, and through Annette requested that he be given an enlarged role in which he would be able to enjoy his personal liberty.

So, in November, 1810, it was arranged that he would be taken in irons before an examining magistrate. Vidocq conveniently escaped, the authorities put on a show of searching for him without finding him, and the underworld celebrated. Better able than before to pursue his new career, Vidocq moved with his mother and Annette to an apartment on the rue Neuve-Saint-François, a little residential street just off the rue Saint-Louis on the Left Bank, perfect for someone with a professional passion for the inconspicuous.

A day or two later he was given his first assignment, the capture of a forger named Watrin who was an expert in counterfeiting bank notes. Captured some months earlier, Watrin had bribed the officials who had arrested him, and they had allowed him to escape. The authorities had no idea where to locate him.

Vidocq made inquiries, and after a few days learned that Watrin had left most of his belongings, including an expensive wardrobe, in a suite of furnished rooms on the boulevard Montparnasse. Vidocq moved into lodgings across the hall with Annette, certain that Watrin would return for his property. One evening he showed up, accompanied by his mistress, but ran off before Vidocq could apprehend him.

He left his mistress behind, and Vidocq promptly established a principle he would follow throughout his career. If the woman cooperated with him, he guaranteed her immunity; if she refused, she would go to prison. She lost no time in telling him where they lived, and Vidocq hurried there, finding Watrin packing a valise preparatory to a hasty departure. Vidocq carried no weapons, but managed to subdue the forger and then hauled him off to the Prefecture.

Watrin, who never knew the real identity of his captor and

therefore could not identify him to other prisoners, spent only a few weeks in jail before being sent to the guillotine, the fate of most thieves. Vidocq was given a handsome cash reward, and his future was now assured.

His success, however, caused problems that would haunt him throughout his career. He had triumphed where the uniformed police of the Prefecture had failed, and they were jealous of him. Their hatred grew as he expanded his activities, and they never forgave him for accomplishing what they could not do.

Vidocq did not regard his achievement as out of the ordinary. On the contrary, it seemed to him that he had merely applied common sense to a problem that plagued the police of France and other nations. Ever since the Middle Ages members of the constabulary in France had worn identifying insignia that over the centuries had become full uniforms; therefore, gendarmes could be recognized on sight.

How much better it would be, Vidocq told his superiors, if police officers assigned to criminal cases wore ordinary civilian attire. He envisaged the formation of a special bureau that would concentrate exclusively on the investigation and detection of crimes. Its membership would be composed of men familiar with the methods and techniques of criminals, who would be aided in their work by files that identified every known robber, thief, forger and confidence man. These special operatives, who have come to be known as detectives, would work independently of the uniformed police, but would have the same authority to make arrests.

The secret police who hunted subversives and terrorists used such a system effectively, Vidocq argued, but the criminal police were hampered because they advertised their presence whenever they went out on a case. The top officials of the Prefecture agreed with him in principle, but his suggestions were premature. Apparently he was told, however, that if he continued to haul in criminals his superiors would give his ideas serious consideration.

Soon he had an opportunity. Two former prison inmates, whom he had known years earlier, asked him to join them in robbing the strongbox that a prominent banker kept in his home. If necessary, the pair said, they would kill the banker. Vidocq duly reported to the Prefecture and was told to prevent the crime.

The day of the caper arrived, and Vidocq kept the police informed of developments by sending them notes, writing them in a toilet and giving them to Annette, who loitered nearby, posing as a prostitute. She was a brunette, and appeared as herself when Vidocq slipped his first note to her. Then she donned a blonde wig and changed her clothes before he gave her the second. This marked the first time that Vidocq utilized a disguise to help the police.

The police were lying in wait at the banker's house when Vidocq and the two criminals appeared. Shots were exchanged, Vidocq pretended he had been shot, and the robbers were captured. They were held in isolation until they were tried and executed so they couldn't reveal to former prisoners that Vidocq had betrayed old comrades.

Sooner or later, Vidocq knew, word would be passed through the Paris underworld that he was working for the police and had the power to make arrests. In order to postpone that day he adopted false identities and disguises that enabled him to function simultaneously on several levels. This complex way of life was primarily responsible for his initial burst of fame, but it is difficult to determine whether he acted deliberately or was forced by circumstances to assume several identities.

Basically he was still Vidocq, the fugitive from justice who lived with Annette and his mother, a drygoods merchant who owned a small shop but who was amenable to occasional participation in illegal enterprises. Twice escaped from the galleys, he remained a hero among the criminal element.

His second identity was that of a fence named Jean-Louis, a sixty-year-old Breton, complete with accent, who had gray hair, drooping mustaches and wore old-fashioned pre-Revolution clothes. Jean-Louis paid higher prices for stolen merchandise than anyone else in the city, was always amenable to a deal and he was willing to help thieves in distress. Vidocq managed to maintain this pose for many years, even though scores of thieves were arrested and convicted, and millions of francs in stolen merchandise were recovered. His ability to keep the character of Jean-Louis alive and active in the face of great obstacles says more for his cleverness than all the panegyrics written about him.

A third identity adopted by Vidocq was that of a burglar and strong-arm man named Jules. A war veteran of about thirty who wore a beard and walked with a pronounced limp, Jules was courageous, always ready to use physical force. His mistress was a vacuous blonde called Marie, a role in which Annette delighted. Obviously she shared Vidocq's pleasure in role-playing. Jules, like Jean-Louis, was responsible for the incarceration of many criminals over the years.

The change in Vidocq's fortunes that began in 1809 is astonishing. For more than twenty years he had been in trouble, thanks to one stupid but compassionate mistake. He had been arrested more times than he could remember and had escaped as frequently. Always on the run, he had assumed many false names and identities as he had hidden and outwitted the authorities.

Now, thanks to chance, he was working for his former enemies, and everything he had done in life had prepared him for his new career. For more than two decades he had devoted his thoughts and energies to the preservation of his precious freedom. Now his natural genius began to emerge, and he became the most innovative law enforcement officer in history. His long experience taught him what needed to be done, and from the beginning he walked with sure, firm steps as he founded a new profession.

He realized from the time he went to work for the authorities that the criminals held an advantage because the gendarmes were ignorant of the law, stupid and vindictive. For every criminal arrested a dozen went free, principally because no concrete evidence had been presented against them in court. Vidocq was determined to acquire evidence by scientific means.

The first case in which he utilized this revolutionary technique occurred in December, 1810, when he became friendly with a thief named Hotot. One morning, when visiting the man's quarters, he noted that the burglar's clothes were wet and his boots were muddy. Knowing it had rained heavily earlier in the day, he went to the Prefecture to inquire whether any major thefts had been reported.

In his autobiography and in scores of interviews, Vidocq later stressed that observation was the first rule of criminal investigation. Arrests would be certain to follow if officials followed appropriate procedures, and the most important was that of keeping their eyes and ears open. Most criminals were careless, he said, and succeeded only because the authorities were even more slipshod. The detective who won convictions saw and listened, then utilized anything he learned that was out of the ordinary and aroused his professional suspicions.

One day Vidocq was told at the Prefecture that there had been a burglary at the home of a count of the Empire, and that the thieves had entered through an open door in a wing of the house that was being reconstructed. He went there, accompanied by several gendarmes, and while making a tour of the property observed the prints left in the soft mud of the garden by a pair of hobnailed boots.

No one had yet thought of using plaster of paris to make reproductions of the prints, so Vidocq instructed two of the policemen to remain in the garden, ordering them to allow no one to tamper with the evidence.

Then he returned to Hotot's apartment, armed with several bottles of wine, which the thief eagerly drank. When the man was intoxicated Vidocq sneaked his boots, which were still drying, out of the place and gave them to a waiting gendarme. The policeman hurried off to the Count's house where it was discovered that the boots fitted the prints exactly.

This information was relayed to Vidocq who immediately placed Hotot under arrest. The evidence was unassailable, and Hotot admitted his guilt, revealing the hiding place of the loot.

Vidocq's summary memorandum of the case, which is still on file in the archives of the Paris police, is laconic and dry. Unlike the flamboyant literary efforts later attributed to him, it confines itself to the facts. This, too, is a major contribution to law enforcement procedures, and when he reached a position of authority he insisted that his subordinates follow his example. Reports were made for two purposes, he believed: the first was the presentation of evidence in a succint, forthright manner, suitable for use in a court of law; second, somewhat less important, but still vital, was the preparation of a permanent record, which included anything unusual in the criminal's technique and any personal idiosyncrasies he exhibited.

Not only was Hotot sent to prison, but he implicated several other members of a ring with which he had been involved. Vidocq conducted an investigation in his Jean-Louis disguise, and when the thieves led him to an old house in which they had concealed their booty, all of them were arrested by policemen who were hiding there. The entire gang was convicted, and Vidocq received an official commendation as well as a substantial reward.

By this time he was well known within the ranks of the police, and aroused the envy of other men who had been used as informers, most of them criminals who worked for the authorities because they would have been sent to prison had they failed to cooperate. Several of them made strenuous efforts to discredit Vidocq, offering him bribes and shady deals if he would close his eyes to the activities of various bands of robbers and burglars. He refused.

What the informers and most members of the uniformed police failed to realize was that Vidocq was not really a criminal. He had spent many months in prison, and his escape record was second to none in France, but he was actually an honest, hardworking man who had exerted great efforts to avoid the consequences of the one foolish act he had perpetrated. Ever since boyhood he had earned his living as a soldier, as a member of a privateer's crew and as an honorable merchant. As yet he had no desire to break the law.

He was a complex man, however, and was difficult to categorize. In 1809 or 1810 — the precise date is uncertain — he received word that his wife, who wanted to remarry, had obtained a divorce. He was free now and could have married the loyal Annette who worked with him so diligently as an unpaid detective's assistant. They had lived together for a number of years, she was on good terms with his mother and it would have been natural for him to make her his wife.

Perhaps the idea of remarriage did not occur to him. But it has also been suggested, in all fairness to him, that Annette may have had a husband somewhere, and that it was she who was in no position to marry.

Certainly Vidocq did not allow his close association with this charming, lovely and faithful young woman to deter him from having other affairs. Like Victor Hugo, who would become his good friend, he was irresistibly drawn to courtesans, actresses, modistes and even street women, provided they were attractive. His greatest weakness, as he readily admitted, was a woman with a pretty face, a svelte figure and a willing disposition.

In several of the novels written under his name, many years later, his protagonists had numerous affairs with attractive women of easy virtue. Vidocq or his ghostwriter indicated that his heroes came from the provinces and were dazzled by the beauty of sophisticated women, but this explanation of his fascination seems glib.

According to some schools of modern psychiatry men like Vidocq are seeking love that has been lacking in their lives, but this analysis does not appear to fit the great detective. Few details of his relationship with his mother are known, but she did not abandon him during the nightmare years when he was in hiding and she shared his hardships with him. She continued to live with him after he gained stature and renown, taking great pride in his accomplishments, and when she died, in 1824, he wrote that she was "the one person in the world who truly cared for me. I loved her equally in return."

He was destined to marry three times and his third wife was almost fanatical in her loyalty to him. He loved her, too, as much as he could love any woman, but that did not deter him from frequently seeking the beds of others. The habits of a lifetime were difficult to break, and it may be that he became so callous he failed to recognize genuine affection when it was offered to him.

Some of his affairs were fleeting, while others lasted for weeks or even months. He sought no particular type and demanded only that a woman be young and pretty. As he became increasingly influential, there were many, particularly women on the fringe of the underworld, who sought his protection and who had affairs with him because of the great power he wielded. When necessary, however, he did not hesitate to pay for a woman's favors, and his sexual desires appear to have been insatiable.

Annette was an appealing figure, and although very little is known about her she captured the imagination of nineteenth-century authors, perhaps because she was a woman of mystery. Two inferior plays were even written about her in the 1860's, both of them failures.

She must have been clever, as she worked with Vidocq frequently, acting as an undercover agent, an active participant when arrests were made and a courier who sometimes placed her own life in jeopardy.

Vidocq later stated that other men found her exceptionally attractive, but that she refused to look at anyone else. She knew better than to expect fidelity in return, however, and like his second and third wives she was tolerant and understanding, giving him the freedom to sleep where he pleased. He always returned to her, and that seems to have satisfied her.

Although deeply attached to her for the better part of a decade, Vidocq never revealed any basic details of their relationship in his autobiography or elsewhere. Annette appeared in his narrative out of nowhere, with no indication of how they had met or what had drawn them together. She was his mistress, sharing his home with him and his mother for a long time before he moved to Paris, and he saw no reason to provide the public with more information.

Annette vanished from his life in the same elusive way. Around the time of Napoleon's downfall, in 1814–1815, she simply disappeared from his story, and he did not mention her again, either as a mistress or as an assistant. Other young women took her place in his home and work, and she seems to have been forgotten.

Dumas, who may have known something of her story, makes a passing reference to her in a letter to Gautier. Referring to one of his own passions of the moment, he declares that he loves her "as much as Vidocq loved his Annette, but alas, like Annette she was married and her husband claimed her." The statement has never been authenticated, and there is no way to verify it. Perhaps it is true, but Dumas was not above inventing a dramatic tale when it suited his purposes.

Eugène Sue thought of using Annette as a major character in a novel but gave up the idea because Vidocq, always happy to boast about his vocational triumphs, was reluctant to talk about her. So she remains an enigma, yet must be given credit for sharing Vidocq's profession in its early, formative stages. She climbed in and out of disguises, kept watch on people he wanted observed and exposed herself to the dangers of retaliation from criminals.

If Vidocq took Annette for granted she was not the only one. By the time he reached his early forties he knew what he wanted, and threw himself into his work with a single-minded devotion. He found himself late in life and was making up for a quarter of a century of lost time. After he conceived the idea of operating as a plainclothes policeman and forming an organization of such persons, he had no time for ordinary pleasures, ordinary loyalties. For the next eighteen years after he joined the Prefecture as an informer, his work was his whole life.

V

By 1811 VIDOCQ was a one-man detective bureau for the Paris police, establishing a formidable record for arrests and convictions. No murderer, robber or forger, no burglar, confidence man or pickpocket in Paris was safe. His identity could no longer be kept secret, and the whole underworld knew, feared and hated the name of Vidocq.

Nevertheless he continued to function, and his success was undiminished. No matter how sly and evasive his opponents were, he was able to outsmart them as he developed and perfected the techniques subsequently used by detectives all over the world.

He not only had a genius for disguise, but was able to teach the art to others. His secret was attention to detail. When he wanted to appear as a laborer he wore only the clothing of the lower-class Paris workingman, complete to underwear, stockings and boots. When he disguised himself as an old man his voice and walk, facial expressions and gestures were those of the elderly. When necessary he dressed as a woman, and the ruse was so successful that, on one occasion, he found it difficult to fend off a pair of would-be lovers.

Playing the role of the character, he stressed, was a more important element of disguise than appearance. He advised the man or woman assuming another identity to become immersed in the personality being adopted. He himself knew the backgrounds of his alter egos, Jean-Louis and Jules, as well as he knew his own and, when pretending to be one of them, he never said anything out of key, never made a false move. There were criminals in Paris who loathed Vidocq but who happily accepted him as either Jean-Louis or Jules.

The simplicity of the techniques he developed was responsible for their success and explains why they are still being utilized a century and a half later. It was Vidocq who turned surveillance into a fine art. Never follow a suspect too closely, he said, and always wear a broad-brimmed hat or similar covering so he doesn't recognize the face of his pursuer.

The officer engaged in surveillance should wear dark, inconspicuous clothing suitable for the area in which the operation takes place. Vidocq suggested that one should never dress as a gentleman in the slums, or as a laborer in a wealthy neighborhood. Also, little touches could be added to confuse the subject and would throw him off guard. The detective should carry several bright scarves in his pocket and should change them frequently. When the subject becomes apprehensive because he believes he is being followed by a man wearing a red scarf, the detective should exchange it for a white scarf that he ties to his hat, and the subject will relax for a time.

When a criminal takes evasive action because he seems certain he is being followed, the watch should be abandoned. If the subject thinks he is being cornered he may become dangerous; if he grows panicky he may flee. It is far better to give up the surveillance, lull him into a false sense of security and then resume it at a later time.

By 1811 Vidocq was actively training other police agents who were working under his supervision. The authorities continued to resist his suggestion that a detective bureau be established, so he went about setting it up informally, in his own way. His success was so great that it was impossible for his superiors to resist his argument that two or three Vidocqs would accomplish more than one, and they not only allowed

him to train others, but put them to work as his immediate
subordinates.

His first assistant was Coco who became adept at recover-
ing stolen property and catching pickpockets. Even more valuable was an ex-convict turned police informer named Riboulet, a husky, hard-drinking giant who could not be trusted
with important secrets because he was inclined to talk out of
turn to his mistress of the moment and he changed mistresses
frequently.

Riboulet had no idea of Vidocq's real identity and knew
him only as Jules. Dogged in pursuit when given a surveillance assignment, Riboulet was particularly appreciated on
occasions when brawn was needed. In December, 1811, Vidocq and Riboulet rounded up several members of a gang of
thieves, and the following month they captured the rest in a
raid on a warehouse. Uniformed police were supposed to join
them in the assault, but arrived late, so Vidocq and Riboulet
were forced to do battle with five criminals. By the time the
gendarmes arrived, they had succeeded in subduing the
thieves.

The top-ranking officials of the Ministry of Police and the
Interior recognized Vidocq's worth by 1812, and he was
given case after case that the uniformed gendarmes were unable to solve. He was building a real career at last and acted
accordingly, working seven days and nights each week,
never taking a holiday. His only relaxations were his affairs
with the endless stream of young women who moved in and
out of his life and his dinners at the new restaurants that
were opening in the city. For the first time in his life Vidocq
was able to afford fine foods and he made it a habit to eat at
least once each day in one of the expensive establishments
that had been opened in the vicinity of the Palais Royal, the
most fashionable part of town.

Only when he was working on an undercover assignment
did he refrain from frequenting these expensive inns. At such
times he ate in slum taverns and was able to simulate an

interest in food that was of inferior quality and also badly cooked. On one occasion a group of burglars suspected he was Vidocq but changed their minds when he ate a stew of dog meat with seeming relish. Vidocq, they had heard, had a refined palate, so they concluded that the man they knew as Jules was one of them, as he claimed.

Paris was swept by crime of unprecedented proportions in 1812, and the authorities struggled against heavy odds to control it. Emperor Napoleon had recruited his largest army, and had marched off on an invasion of Russia, almost denuding France of young, able-bodied men. Most of the gendarmes who patrolled the streets of the capital were middle aged, no longer able to cope with agile, experienced criminals, and the underworld enjoyed a bonanza.

The problem was compounded by red tape. The Prefecture was divided into twenty-four districts, each jealous of its area of jurisdiction, and a lack of liaison between district commanders made it possible for a criminal to remain at liberty indefinitely merely by changing his address frequently from one district to another.

Vidocq was aware of this weakness in the system and proposed a remedy. In the autumn of 1812 he renewed his suggestion to the Ministry that a plainclothes bureau be formed, and he stressed that it should function in all districts, including the suburbs. He wanted to call this new organization the Sûreté, or security police, and he recommended that it report directly to the Prefect, the head of the entire Paris police department.

The commissaires, or district commanders, saw their own authority being usurped and protested violently. By this time the Ministry was desperate, however, and the record Vidocq had established in the past three years was so impressive that his plan was approved. Comte Jean Dubois, the Prefect, as chief of police, signed the order establishing the Brigade de la Sûreté in late October, 1812.

Vidocq was authorized to hire eight men, their real identities known only to him. He was given his own headquarters, in an old, three-story building at Number 6, Petite rue Sainte-Anne, near one óf the city's loveliest churches, Sainte-Chapelle. Work and conference rooms occupied the ground floor; Vidocq made his own headquarters on the second floor and stored his files there; on the top floor was a dormitory his men could use when necessary, a small kitchen and a dining room.

The wife of one of his men was hired to cook meals for members of the Brigade de la Sûreté, who were paid their living expenses but received no wages. Instead they were given a fee for each arrest they made. All were men with criminal records, which infuriated the uniformed police, but the Chief of the new Sûreté ignored their protests. His men were thoroughly familiar with the tricks of the underworld, and he wanted immediate results. He expressed a willingness, however, to accept two volunteer recruits from the uniformed ranks and to put them through a training course of one year. At the end of that time, he believed, they would know enough about criminal techniques to be of use to him.

Comte Dubois accepted this suggestion. After Vidocq established his original force of ex-convicts, he added to it annually by promoting non-convicts he had trained himself. By 1817 thirty detectives worked full time for the Brigade de la Sûreté.

Vidocq was given the rank, salary and prerogatives of a commissaire, which further angered the district commanders. He quickly advanced beyond their level, however, and by 1814, he was a Deputy Prefect, in a position to call on the uniformed police for help when he wished. The rivalry was so intense, however, that the new Sûreté rarely asked the gendarmes for assistance.

From the outset Vidocq established strict rules and procedures and displayed a genius for organization. His eight subordinates used aliases and were encouraged to uŭlize several identities, as their chief did. Word was passed through the underworld that informers would be well paid and their identities would remain secret. Only one room at the Sûreté's headquarters was open to visitors. Prisoners were taken to windowless, escape-proof rooms in the cellar, where it was said they were forced to make confessions of their crimes.

Vidocq preferred to abstain from torture, however. He knew that even the most hardened criminals would cooperate if they had something to gain and from the beginning he made deals, obtaining lighter sentences and even winning immediate freedom for those who gave him information that would lead to bigger quarry.

The file system instituted by Vidocq was one of his most impressive innovations. Modern police everywhere rely heavily on files, and the National Crime Information Center operated by the Federal Bureau of Investigation is simply the largest and most complex of computer-operated criminal files that are deemed essential in virtually every country on earth.

Until Vidocq set up the Sûreté's files, however, such a system was unknown. Each Paris district kept records of sorts, but these stacks of paper were a jumbled mess that had no practical value. Vidocq himself had a phenomenal memory and he not only could recognize a criminal he had not seen in twenty years, but could remember the various misdeeds the man had committed. Others lacked his talent, however, and he set up his files on the very day he opened his headquarters.

Full records were kept on all known members of the underworld, major and minor, with whom the Sûreté came in contact. Aliases were listed, and a physical description of the criminal was included. The information on his card included all previous convictions, and, most important, his methods of operation.

Vidocq appears to have been the first police official ever to realize that individual criminals often gave themselves away by the repeated use of identifiable techniques. The leader of a gang of highly successful burglars, for example, only robbed ground floor apartments, gaining admission by using a thin blade of strong, Spanish steel with which he pried open a window. Released from prison after serving a sentence of eight years, this individual became active again and his special technique was responsible for his arrest on new charges. The evidence against him was overwhelming, and he was again convicted.

Members of the Brigade de la Sûreté were directed to write daily reports on their activities, and within six months of the organization's formation Vidocq was granted the right to add four clerks to his payroll, their function being that of keeping the index files and making records that all members of the Bureau could use.

By the autumn of 1813 Vidocq's files filled one room, and thereafter they continued to expand even more rapidly. Many criminals came to believe he was endowed with a special magic that enabled him to know their past histories, and he did not disillusion them. He permitted the uniformed police to use his files, which they did with increasing frequency, although they continued to criticize his employment of men with criminal records.

Many years later, in a treatise actually written in his own hand, Vidocq defended himself:

During the twenty years I spent at the head of the Sûreté my staff was composed, in the main, of ex-convicts, often even escaped prisoners. I preferred to choose men whose bad records had given them a certain celebrity.

Well! I often gave these men the most delicate missions. They had considerable sums of money to deliver to the uniformed police or the prison offices; they took part in operations in which they could easily have laid hands on large amounts, and not one of them — not a single one! — betrayed my trust.

It has been my experience that when the Prefecture has found it necessary to take action against Sûreté agents for theft, these persons invariably were men who had come to us through the ranks of the uniformed police and had no previous criminal records. The former criminal who is given the opportunity to hold an honest post and regain the respect of society is so grateful for this chance that he walks the straightest of straight paths. Every former criminal who was employed by me repaid his debt to society many times over.

The realm of Napoleon crumbled rapidly after the remnants of his battered army limped home from the catastrophic Russian campaign, but the Emperor continued to take an interest in everything of consequence that took place in the world he still ruled. When Vidocq's success was called to his attention late in 1813, he wrote the Chief of the Brigade de la Sûreté a letter of commendation. A few days later Vidocq was awarded a medal and a purse containing one hundred gold francs, the equivalent of $4000 a century and a half later. Whether Napoleon honored him in person or made the presentation through the Ministry is not known, but the effect was the same. The unorthodox labors of a new type of law enforcement official had won recognition at the highest level, and the commissaires prudently lowered their voices.

On December 17, 1813, the bureau achieved its greatest triumph in its short history. A scant four months before Napoleon was forced by his enemies to abdicate and was sent to Elba in exile, he signed a decree making the Brigade de la Sûreté a national security force, and from that day down to the present it has proudly been called the Sûreté Nationale. Vidocq promptly established branches in Arras, Brest, Toulon and Lyons. It may have been accidental that he elected to set up operations in the town of his birth and the three cities where he had encountered his own greatest difficulties with the law, but that is unlikely. Perhaps he was thumbing his nose at the authorities who had made his life miserable, but at the same time he had chosen other centers of crime almost as notorious as Paris.

Unfortunately, the chain of command outlined in the original directive was hazy. The Sûreté in Paris was required to report to the Prefecture, and the branches were under the direct supervision of the uniformed police in those communities. Vidocq spent his entire career in the Sûreté trying to create a truly national bureau under his own, centralized control. It was a nuisance and a waste of time when tracking a criminal who traveled from Lyons to Paris, to work with the gendarmes of several cities and towns, and occasionally a suspect vanished.

Rather than subject his men to this frustration, Vidocq sometimes "forgot" to notify the various authorities of his bureau's activities, preferring to wait until he obtained his needed evidence and arrested his suspects. This discourtesy further estranged the uniformed police, and his unbroken string of successes irritated envious officials everywhere. Vidocq had not yet been pardoned for his own criminal offense, the forgery he had committed in his youth, and many conservative policemen insisted that he could not be trusted.

Had he been willing to let the record being amassed by the Sûreté speak for itself, the opposition to him might have subsided. But that was not his way. After spending the better part of his life as a fugitive he had risen high in society in early middle age, and he wanted the world to know it. Modesty was not one of his attributes, and in the spring of 1814, when the victorious Allies put Louis XVIII on the throne, the returning Bourbons were greeted by a flood of pamphlets enumerating the triumphs of the Sûreté Nationale.

Two of Napoleon's closest associates managed to keep their positions. Foreign Minister Talleyrand and Minister of Police and the Interior Fouché were wily politicians who could shift with the political winds in order to keep their high positions. Vidocq ranked far lower in the power structure, to be sure, but he also survived, probably because of his complete lack of interest in politics. He didn't care who sat on the throne provided he was given the authority to catch criminals.

The restored Bourbons were inefficient and shortsighted,

incapable of turning back the clock and changing the new society that Napoleon had created. They were willing to tolerate many reforms, provided their own security was not threatened, so the Sûreté Nationale continued to function. The glowing pamphlets, undoubtedly written and printed at Vidocq's personal expense, duly impressed Louis XVIII and his strong-willed brother, the future Charles X. Not only did Vidocq remain in office, but between May, 1814, and the following March, when Napoleon escaped from Elba and rallied his Grand Army, Vidocq's little detective force grew to sixty men.

Others could raise armies, march and counter-march. He devoted himself exclusively to the task of apprehending criminals, and the more chaotic domestic conditions became, the more he seemed to accomplish. There is no mention in his autobiography of the Hundred Days, Napoleon's final defeat at Waterloo or the second restoration of the Bourbons.

The monarchs of Europe converged on Paris when Napoleon was sent off to his final place of exile, the island of St. Helena, and the city overflowed with wealthy, noble visitors. More than three hundred gentlemen formed the entourage accompanying Tsar Alexander of Russia, for example, and the underworld looked forward to a gloriously profitable summer.

Vidocq had other ideas, and for once the commissaires, eager to keep their own positions, willingly cooperated with him. He put scores of uniformed police into civilian clothes, placing them under the command of his own men, and the distinguished visitors were not molested. All known burglars and pickpockets in Paris were arrested, escorted to Orléans and kept there until the festivities in the capital came to an end.

In the autumn of 1815 Vidocq received his reward. He was granted an audience by Louis XVIII who reconfirmed him as Chief of the Brigade de la Sûreté and Deputy Prefect. His enemies had hoped to persuade the new monarch to abolish the revolutionary detective bureau, but Vidocq acted first, and his foes were unable to influence the crown in favor of his dismissal.

Forty years old in 1815, Vidocq was now a man of consequence. He moved with his mother to a substantial house, which he purchased, and he continued to dine in the restaurants near the Palais Royal with a succession of young courtesans and actresses.

On these occasions Vidocq wore handsomely tailored clothes, rode in a carriage pulled by a matched team of horses and carried a walking stick with a solid gold handle. At the same time, however, he did not hesitate to descend into the underworld, and he still maintained his disguises as Jean-Louis and Jules. He asked nothing of his men that he was unwilling to do himself and he continued to arrest more criminals than any of his subordinates in the Sûreté.

Vidocq was so conscientious that many criminals abandoned Paris and moved their base of operations to Brussels, Geneva and other cities. So many stories were told about the treatment of underworld members at "Number Six" that many who were apprehended and taken there for questioning voluntarily confessed. Vidocq deliberately spread the word that he and his men were infallible, and whenever the Sûreté scored another triumph the newspapers played it up. The Chief of the Sûreté admittedly enjoyed the favorable publicity but insisted he had only one aim: that of making the underworld uneasy.

His critics had one legitimate cause for complaint: Vidocq lived far beyond the modest salary he earned as a police officer. it may be, as his enemies openly charged years later, that he accepted large sums from wealthy citizens in return for alleged special "protection" from burglars and robbers, but this claim was never proved.

When he was an old man Vidocq finally admitted that throughout his long career he had earned substantial sums on the side as a moneylender, but he took pains to point out that there was nothing illegal in this activity. He loaned money at rates more favorable than those given by most private bankers, so his argument that he was performing a legitimate service was valid.

What he failed to mention was that his method of collection was unique. Vidocq was more tolerant than the private bankers who sued clients unable or unwilling to repay their debts on time. In forty years Vidocq went to court only a few times. He dealt fairly with those who were honest, but was unscrupulous in his treatment of anyone who tried to cheat him.

Sometimes, when a client lacked the funds to repay a loan, Vidocq was willing to carry the burden for years. But there were many wealthy noblemen who were careless and had no intention of repaying the funds they had borrowed to see them through a period of temporary financial embarrassment. Vidocq had his own way of dealing with such persons. After the borrower received several solemn warnings his house was burgled, and only items of great value such as jewelry, paintings, tapestries and clocks disappeared.

These items were sold through underworld fences, and presumably Vidocq pocketed the profits. Certainly he regarded the accounts of these delinquent borrowers as closed. No one has ever known whether these burglaries were perpetrated by members of the Sûreté who were experienced in the field, or by underworld characters recruited for the purpose. If the victim had the temerity to report his losses to the authorities, he could be sure that the Sûreté would take charge of the case, ultimately informing him that it had not been possible to trace his missing property.

In his professional life he was incorruptible. The leaders of several gangs of robbers and burglars tried at one time or another to bribe him in return for dropping the charges against them; they were given increased sentences for their pains. He was equally zealous in his insistence that the members of his staff stay honest. Aware of the hostility of the uniformed police to a bureau made up mostly of ex-convicts, he realized that his enemies would seize every opportunity to embarrass the Sûreté. So he made a rule and insisted that it be enforced: any member of the bureau who accepted a bribe or personal favor was dismissed instantly from the force.

Not even Vidocq's worst enemies could accuse him of cowardice. By 1815 the entire underworld knew he was the head of a new bureau that used strange, unorthodox means of bringing criminals to justice, and there were many who swore they would kill him. At the insistence of the Prefect he was accompanied everywhere by two bodyguards when he went abroad as himself, but he found the presence of his escort irksome, and knew he had to perform a dramatic deed to prove to the criminals that he was not afraid of them.

For a long time he had wanted to attend the fettering of chain gang prisoners at Bicêtre, a prison just outside Paris, believing he might recognize men who had committed crimes in addition to those for which they were being sent to the galleys. Neither the Prefect nor the Ministry would grant him the necessary permission to be present at one of these occasions, for the simple reason that the convicts, hysterical at the prospect of spending years in chains, might well murder him if he descended into the courtyard with them.

But he persisted in his demand, and late in 1815 his request was granted. As anticipated, the prisoners staged a near riot when they learned the identity of the man in black who strolled into the prison courtyard among them.

The courage displayed by Vidocq on this occasion was remarkable and can be appreciated only in relation to the time in which he lived. Justice was still rough, and criminals were sent to their death for committing crimes that today would be regarded as minor. Thieves and swindlers, for instance, were sent to the guillotine as a matter of course.

Convicts were treated like animals, and repeated offenders were subjected to brutalities that would be regarded as shocking in the late twentieth century. Criminals were beaten, abused and forced to live according to sub-human standards as a matter of course. Only after the vigorous campaigns conducted by such authors as Sue, Hugo and Zola, all of them influenced by Vidocq, did conditions improve.

Before the actual fettering took place the convicts were herded into a central yard where many of them became hysterical. It was not unusual for a prisoner to run amok, committing mayhem and even murder, but the authorities did not care. If a convict died there would be one less to feed slops to.

By going into the yard Vidocq subjected himself to grave personal danger. He could be stabbed, strangled or beaten to death before the guards could intervene, and the criminal code of silence would shield the identities of his killers.

He was well aware of the risks, but nevertheless took them. Certainly he must have remembered his own fettering on two separate occasions. According to Vidocq's autobiography he made a stirring speech that silenced the mob, but even in a melodramatic play no actor would have spoken such stilted words. A more sober account of the occasion states that the prisoners filed past Vidocq as they went to that portion of the yard where their chains would be attached to them. They were still unfettered, so any one of them could have lunged at him, and, if a fight had developed, there is no doubt he could have been killed before the guards could have intervened. Théophile Gautier, who described the incident in an essay, said that Vidocq stood with folded arms, his manner cold and forbidding as he stared at each prisoner in turn. No hand was raised against him.

The incident served its double purpose. Vidocq let the underworld know in no uncertain terms that he was not afraid of potential assassins and, in the process, he recognized several men who had committed multiple crimes. Subsequently they were tried again and given increased sentences.

His presence in the courtyard also gave him an opportunity

he was quick to grasp. A number of the convicts asked him to deliver farewell messages to their families or women with whom they had been living, and because he could sympathize with these unfortunate wretches he quickly agreed.

Always on the lookout for Sûreté recruits, he regarded some of these convicts as promising and maintained contacts with them. Ultimately he won the release of three prisoners and promptly gave them jobs as detectives. Their loyalty to him was unwavering.

The session was so profitable that he made it a habit to attend fetterings regularly, and at no time was he attacked. The convicts came to accept his presence, and when he missed a session because he was occupied elsewhere the prisoners were upset. On one occasion, according to Gautier, they rioted and demanded that the chaining be postponed until the Chief of the Sûreté could be there.

The immediate result of Vidocq's visit to Bicêtre became evident as soon as he returned to Paris. Ignoring the advice of his superiors, he dismissed his bodyguards and never called on them for help again. This gesture was deliberate: he understood the mind of the criminal and wanted to impress on the underworld that their enemy was omnipotent as well as fearless. His battle was half-won if a robber, burglar or confidence man was convinced that the Sûreté would track him down and catch him.

It was not accidental that by 1817, a scant five years after the detective bureau was founded, it was responsible for more arrests and convictions annually than any other police force in France.

VI

Vidocq's place in history would have been secure, even without the Brigade de la Sûreté, had he confined himself to the development of a new type of police officer, the detective, and to his ultimate establishment of the world's first private detective agency with his services and those of his assistants available for hire. But his greatest contribution to crime detection was his passionate belief, which he practiced, that the criminal-catcher needed to rely on science for success.

As has already been noted, he instituted a new type of readily accessible filing system that identified the individual criminal and explained his techniques. All new members of the Sûreté were carefully instructed, too, in his system of surveillance. The simple precautions he utilized were so successful that within a few years they were being imitated by plainclothes police throughout Europe, Great Britain and the United States.

Crime, as Vidocq noted and as law enforcement officials everywhere well know, is a communicable disease. An ax murder often is followed by others; when a kidnaping is publicized, a rash of similar crimes breaks out. Most criminals lack imagination, Vidocq said, and tend to be imitative.

This theory was confirmed in France in the years immediately following the downfall of Napoleon and the return of the Bourbons. The country had been bled of manpower and money by the Emperor's wars, and financial conditions were chaotic. Overnight there was an epidemic of forgeries and counterfeiting.

The principal victims were the private bankers of Paris and other cities. These men issued handsomely inscribed documents ordering their vault keepers to pay cash to the bearer in the amount written on the face of the paper. These documents were the forerunners of the present check.

Clever criminals bought such documents from individuals to whom they had been issued, paying slightly more than the face value, and then changed the amount of the payments to be made by the vault keeper. The bankers were losing millions of francs each year, and the forgers were difficult to track.

At the same time there was an outbreak of counterfeiting on a large scale. In spite of the political upheavals the French economy was continuing to expand, and many new companies were being organized. These firms, whose ambitions were greater than their cash reserves, financed themselves by issuing bonds that paid interest of 2 to 3 per cent, regarded at the time as sound investments. Thousands of people who bought such bonds, however, soon discovered that they had purchased counterfeits and that the salesmen from whom they had bought the bonds had vanished.

Vidocq waged an unrelenting campaign against forgers and counterfeiters and sent many to prison, but there were too many new specialists in these crimes for his small organization to keep up with them. So he decided to attack the problem at the source.

At his instigation two chemists went to work on the problem in 1817 and by the following year they had developed a new type of paper that had been treated with chemicals: no erasures or alterations could be made in the printing without smearing the ink and making the document illegible. At the same time they invented a new ink that could not be erased or changed in any way. When something was written with this ink it was indelible.

Vidocq paid the chemists flat fees for their labors and took out patents on the paper and ink in his own name. As soon as he secured these rights he opened a small factory on the outskirts of Paris to manufacture the paper and the ink.

Thereafter when forgery and counterfeiting cases were called to his attention, he urged the fleeced bankers and the outraged company executives whose bonds had been copied to buy his paper and ink, thus guaranteeing their future financial safety. Within two years the factory had to move to larger quarters. Eventually Vidocq leased his patents to other manufacturers, obtaining a royalty in return, and his earnings from these sources helped make him wealthy, enabling him to live in the style to which he had so rapidly accustomed himself.

He was in a perfect position to recommend the use of his special paper and equally special ink and he did not hesitate to take full advantage of his opportunities. He was criticized by officials of the uniformed police, but his activities were legal, and they had no way of forcing him to dispose of his holdings. And, as Victor Hugo pointed out in a newspaper article written in defense of Vidocq in 1829, there was a sharp decrease in altered and forged documents when bankers and the proprietors of new companies began to use the special paper and ink. In the mid-1860's the French government began to use his ink in the printing of paper money, and it may be poetic justice that nothing was paid to his estate for the privilege.

Vidocq was one of the first to recognize the use of fingerprints as a means of making positive identifications of criminals and he made significant progress in a field later to become primary in police and investigative work everywhere. It is unfortunate that, given his penchant for scientific methods, he stopped short of his goal.

The utilization of fingerprints as a means of identification is as old as civilization itself. Prints may be found in lieu of signatures on clay tablets used as business contracts in ancient Babylon, and on the face of a cliff in Nova Scotia, a prehistoric Indian artist drew a hand with crudely marked prints. In the Orient fingerprints were impressed on business documents as early as the T'ang dynasty in eighth-century China.

The modern history of fingerprinting begins in 1684, when Dr. Nehemiah Grew mentioned the ridge patterns that appear on fingertips in the course of a lecture he delivered before the Royal College of Physicians in London. But a scientific approach had to be made before fingerprints could be used on a broad scale as a means of identification.

The science of fingerprinting grew out of the invention of the microscope. The first, crude microscope using a single lens for the purpose of magnification was invented by Antony van Leeuwenhoek of Delft in the mid-seventeenth century, and in 1684, Christian Huygens improved on the original with the invention of a simple but highly effective two lens microscope.

It was only two years later, in 1686, that Marcello Malpighi, Professor of Anatomy at the University of Bologna, used the Huygens microscope and wrote a treatise on "certain elevated ridges" that were "drawn out into loops and spirals" at the ends of fingers. If he realized that no two persons had the same patterns on their fingers he did not mention it, and it did not occur to him that these markings could be utilized as a means of identification.

The new science languished for 137 years. In 1823 a Professor of Anatomy at the University of Breslau, John Evangelist Purkinje, published a thesis in which he noted that there was a "diversity of ridge patterns, especially on the last phalanx of each finger." His greatest contribution was that of developing a loose system of identification by distinguishing nine different types or varieties of patterns.

Purkinje's work created no ripples anywhere and having been written only for the edification of a few colleagues, it was unknown in other circles. There is no reason to be-

lieve that Vidocq had either heard of Purkinje's thesis or read
it.

By this time, however, many people in Europe were becoming aware of fingerprints, even if they didn't know how
to use them. In 1858, the year after Vidocq's death, Sir William J. Herschel, the chief administrative officer in Bengal,
India, insisted that Indians affix their fingerprints as well as
their signatures to all contracts.

The honor of installing the first formal system of fingerprint
files as an official method of criminal identification goes to
Juan Vucetich, an Argentinian police official, who put his
method into effect in 1891. A combination of circumstances
prevented Vidocq from doing the same thing a half-century
earlier.

Familiar with a much improved Huygens microscope before 1820, Vidocq was fascinated by the ridge patterns found
on fingertips. In the late 1820's he discussed them with Hugo
and Dumas, both of whom wrote that he believed they could
be used as a means of identification. He was mystified, however, by the means that might be used to classify an individual's prints, and Dumas wrote that "Vidocq is in hopes he
can persuade an eminent physician to share his enthusiasm
for this novel method of identification."

Apparently Vidocq's efforts to communicate his zeal were
not successful. Meanwhile he made his own experiments,
bullying inmates of Bicêtre and other prisons into allowing
him to make fingertip prints. He quickly discovered that ordinary ink was unsatisfactory for the purpose because it
smudged. Naturally, he tried his own indelible ink, which
left stains on the fingers of convicts that required weeks to
eradicate. He discovered that his ink dried so quickly on the
fingers that it left too faint a print.

He continued to experiment until he left the Sûreté, for the
first time, in 1827, and he failed to learn what Vucetich found
out in Argentina, that printer's ink was perfect for the purpose. In 1826 Vidocq tried placing the fingerprints of con-

victs on damp clay and he was delighted that the markings were clearly legible. But he was already operating in offices overflowing with records and could not contemplate a filing system of cumbersome clay tablets that would require more space than his superiors were willing to give him.

During his second term at the Sûreté, 1830 to 1833, and throughout his career as a private detective, Vidocq continued to believe that fingerprints could be used as a means of identification. He discussed the matter on various occasions at dinner with Balzac and with Sue, both of whom duly recorded his comments.

Until the end of his life he continued to believe that fingerprinting would be a positive means of identifying criminals. In 1845 when he visited England at the age of seventy, he discussed the subject at some length in interviews he gave to a reporter from the *Times* of London and a correspondent for the *New York Post*.

Certainly it is not too much to claim that his persisting enthusiasm for the science of fingerprinting kept the subject alive, and the rapid developments in the years following his death may have been sparked, at least in part, by his own stubborn faith.

His instincts for the scientific investigation of crimes were almost infallible. In his day there were no ballistics laboratories and no ballistics experts, but he was a pioneer in that field, too.

In 1822 Paris was electrified by a juicy scandal when the Comtesse Isabelle d'Arcy, a beauty more than twenty-five years younger than her husband, was found dead in her bed, with a bullet in her forehead. The uniformed police could find no clues, so the Sûreté was called in, and Vidocq quickly established that the Comtesse had an Italian lover named Deloro.

The Comte d'Arcy was arrested, although he claimed he was innocent. Vidocq had the feeling that d'Arcy had not killed his wife, even though she had given him cause. As he later explained to Dumas, although the Comte's wife had been unfaithful to him, the old gentleman's personality was not that of a murderer.

In the original charge it was stated that the shot "probably" had been fired by one of a pair of duelling pistols that belonged to d'Arcy. As one of the first steps in his subsequent investigation Vidocq took the revolutionary step of examining the pistols, and in his report he stated that if one had been fired it had then been cleaned.

Then, before the Comtesse was buried, Vidocq persuaded a physician who was a friend to remove the bullet from her forehead. This had to be done secretly, as there would have been a great public uproar if the act had been publicized. Autopsies were almost unknown in the early part of the nineteenth century, and only since the French Revolution had cadavers from the morgue been provided, quietly, for medical students to dissect and study. Even then the bodies were those of poverty-stricken men and women who had no known relatives. The upper classes would have been shocked had it been known that a doctor had cut into the head of the dead Comtesse and removed the bullet.

Once Vidocq was in possession of the fatal bullet, he proved to his own satisfaction that it could not have been fired by one of d'Arcy's duelling pistols. Although it was misshapen after striking a bone, it was still far too large to have been fired by the Comte's pistols, the only weapons he possessed.

The next step was typical of Vidocq's style of operation. He made it his immediate business to discover the whereabouts of Deloro, the Comtesse's lover, and found he was in Paris. Isabelle d'Arcy had been a tall, slender redhead, and Vidocq went to an actress he had known intimately, also a tall, slender redhead. He explained what he wanted and paid for her services.

The actress saw to it that she struck up an acquaintance with Deloro, and a few days later she became his mistress.

He had no known means of support but early every afternoon he went off to dine with several male friends. The redhead slept late one morning and soon after Deloro's departure she admitted Vidocq into his apartment.

Searching the place without a warrant was a technicality that Vidocq frequently shrugged off. It didn't take him long to find the evidence he was seeking, a large pistol and a hidden box containing a number of valuable rings, bracelets and necklaces.

Hurrying to the prison, Vidocq showed the jewelry to d'Arcy who immediately identified the objects as gifts he had given to his wife since their marriage five years earlier. Vidocq knew he was on the right track.

He raced to his own office at Number Six and there he matched the lethal bullet with the pistol he had taken from Deloro's apartment. Even though the nose had been squashed, the pellet roughly fitted into the chamber of the gun.

Only one step remained. Vidocq changed into his disguise as Jean-Louis and went to a prominent fence who dealt in stolen diamonds and other gems. Pretending that Deloro owed him money, Vidocq tricked the fence into admitting that only a few days earlier he had purchased a diamond ring from the Italian. Now Vidocq had all the evidence he needed.

When Deloro returned to his apartment that evening he expected to find his new red-haired mistress awaiting him, but instead he was greeted by Vidocq and two of his Sûreté assistants. Shown the jewelry, the bullet that fitted his pistol and told that it was known he had sold a diamond ring a few days earlier, Deloro promptly confessed: it was he who had murdered the Comtesse and then had stolen her jewelry.

Vidocq personally escorted him to the prison, where he was charged with the murder. Comte d'Arcy was released that same night, and became one of Vidocq's most enthusiastic supporters. Deloro went to the guillotine.

According to Dumas, who may or may not have been taking poetic license with the facts, Vidocq made it his business to introduce the accommodating redheaded actress to the Comte. She became his mistress and lived in luxury, thereby winning her reward for the role she had played; and d'Arcy had a lovely companion who provided him with consolation for the tragedies he had suffered.

Dumas, concerned only with the human elements of the story, paid no attention to the most significant aspect of the case: what established Deloro as the murderer was that the death bullet matched his pistol. Vidocq's excursion into ballistics was primitive but it solved the case.

Gradually, under his direction, the Sûreté developed more refined ballistics techniques, and a new science was established. Certainly Vidocq would have been pleased had he known of the great ballistics laboratories at the Sûreté Nationale, the FBI, Scotland Yard and other investigative organizations in the late twentieth century.

Vidocq was a pioneer, too, in using blood tests to help solve crimes. Very little was known about blood groups in the 1820's, but Vidocq nevertheless introduced new techniques in a field that no one before him had explored.

In 1825 another murder excited the citizens of Paris. A self-made millionaire named Matthieu was killed in a large house near the Palais Royal where he lived alone. Somewhat eccentric after his retirement, Matthieu had filled his home with expensive bric-a-brac, so it was impossible to determine what objects, if any, had been removed from the cluttered house. From the outset robbery was suspected as a motive.

Still powerful in spite of his advanced years, Matthieu had fought hard with his killer, and the smashed furniture in his study indicated there had been a wild battle. Vidocq, who made the investigation himself, discovered large bloodstains on the hardwood floor of the study, on the door latches and on the marble staircase leading from the study to the ground floor. He took care to preserve these stains.

Then, changing into his disguise as the brash Jules, he prowled the taverns, inns and other haunts favored by the underworld as he searched for a man, physically strong, who had been battered in a recent fight. After roaming from place to place for hours he found a man who fitted the description, a thief named Richard. Pretending to be drunk, Vidocq picked a quarrel with him, and soon they were trading punches. When they began to smash furniture and break up the tavern, the proprietor called the gendarmes. Richard and Jules were hauled off to jail for disturbing the peace, and, just before they were separated, the disguised Vidocq took a clean handkerchief from his pocket and astonished Richard by wiping a cut he had reopened over the thief's eye.

Released as soon as he established his identity, Vidocq returned to his headquarters, where he made a simple test. Experiments with various chemicals had shown that when dried blood was smeared with certain chemical substances it turned different shades, depending on the individual. One man's blood became a bright crimson, while another might show up a pale pink.

After treating the handkerchief with chemicals Vidocq returned to the house of Matthieu, where he made similar tests on the bloodstains found on the door latches and floors. They turned the same shade as the marks on the handkerchief.

These crude tests were not admissible as evidence in court because they were too imprecise, but Vidocq had proved to his own satisfaction that Richard was the killer of the old man. Returning to the jail the following morning as himself, he confronted Richard, who was awed when he was told the results of the blood tests. Vidocq's reputation was so great by this time that the cowed thief confessed that he had murdered Matthieu. Less than a month later he went to the guillotine.

This case received widespread publicity in the press, the editors of newspapers and their avid readers finding something miraculous in the solution of a murder case by making tests of blood smears with chemicals. The Richard case received wide attention abroad, and soon physicians and chemists in the German states and Great Britain, as well as in France, were experimenting with mixtures of chemicals on blood. Thanks to the imaginative initiative of Vidocq, another scientific method of investigating crimes was inaugurated.

These successes inspired Vidocq to remark at dinner with Dumas, one night in the spring of 1829, that the day would come when all objects found near the scene of a crime would be subjected to examination under a microscope. The author duly wrote an article on the subject, and it was published in a newspaper, but no one, including Vidocq himself, followed up on the suggestion.

The idea was regarded as bizarre, and the better part of a century would pass before the microscope would become a basic tool in crime laboratories.

VII

IN THE YEARS immediately following the restoration of the Bourbons, the Sûreté Nationale became increasingly respected as its reputation grew. In 1817 Vidocq thought the time was ripe for making a major change in the status of his subordinates and, late in the year, he formally petitioned the Ministry of Police and the Interior for the right to pay salaries to twenty-four of his senior agents.

The uniformed police fought the innovation, insisting it was outrageous to even consider the idea of making ex-convicts full-time civil servants. They were overruled, however, and twenty-four Sûreté detectives joined their chief on the government payroll.

Elated by his success, Vidocq took another bold step that many of his contemporaries regarded as shocking. Ever since he had founded the bureau he had received informal help from one or another of his mistresses who had assisted him in the solution of many crimes. In 1818 Vidocq decided to add several women to the Sûreté as agents in their own right. Their expenses would be paid and, like the male agents, they would receive a reward whenever the evidence they accumulated led to an arrest and conviction. He proposed that women agents be denied only the power to make arrests because, he argued, it might be too dangerous for them.

The uniformed police were stunned, promptly claiming that Vidocq was merely planning to hire prostitutes with whom he himself was having affairs. Certainly there was a degree of validity to the charge: Vidocq freely admitted that he slept with many women. He replied to his critics, however, that respectable women would serve no useful purpose in the Sûreté and that only those at home in the underworld would be of help to him.

Whether he actually petitioned the Ministry for the right to hire women agents is unclear. Inasmuch as he did his own recruiting and was placed under no restrictions, he may have already had the right to hire anyone he wished. All that can be said with certainty is that, beginning in 1818, he did employ women, the first ever to serve anywhere as detectives.

Vidocq's literary friends subsequently went overboard on the subject and, in turn, inspired lesser members of their profession who filled the magazines of Paris with short stories and articles about the alleged exploits of the agents in skirts. Virtually all of these accounts were lurid and may be dismissed as romantic rubbish.

The facts are difficult to unearth. All Sûreté agents, regardless of whether they were male or female, were semi-anonymous in accordance with Vidocq's conviction that they could function only if their identities remained unknown in the underworld. Even when writing about them after his retirement, he continued to cloak them in mystery.

One of the first of the women employed by him was known only as the Nun, a nickname she acquired because she sometimes donned a habit and pretended she lived in one of the convents located in the slum districts. First sent to prison at the age of twelve as a thief, she had spent more time behind bars than in the outer world since that time and was in her late twenties when she went to work for the Sûreté.

On several occasions when Vidocq went out on a case in disguise she accompanied him, masquerading as his wife and, no doubt, conveniently sleeping with him. She was an expert on burglars and burglary techniques and was directly responsible for the arrest of a number of thieves. Vidocq later gave her credit for breaking up a ring that had stolen loot worth hundreds of thousands of francs from wealthy families.

Another of his recruits was known only as Violette, but her real identity appears to have been known to Hugo and Dumas, and with good reason. She was one of the highest-priced prostitutes in Paris, sometimes working out of one of the city's most expensive brothels, sometimes appearing at restaurants and the theater in the company of her many admirers. Dumas openly admitted he knew her, and Hugo hinted that he was acquainted with her.

Confidence men who fleeced the wealthy and prominent were not easy to trace because their victims often were reluctant to notify the authorities that they had been fooled. Only when they suffered staggering losses did they come forward, and often their revelations proved to have been made too late, the villains having fled the country.

Vidocq believed that the prevention of confidence games was the best defense against it, and Violette became a valuable subordinate and ally in his war on this type of crime. The confidence man habitually enjoyed high living, wore expensive clothes and dined at the best restaurants. Members of the breed liked to be seen in the company of beautiful women, too, and were not above boasting about their exploits to the type of young woman who, in a later era, would be known as a call girl.

Violette was a sympathetic listener who had a knack for persuading men to talk, and she was endowed with a good memory. The identities of her clients were confidential, so it was safe for Vidocq to visit her at regular intervals. After a meeting with her, during which he probably mixed business and pleasure, male agents visited various confidence men who were either placed under arrest or, if evidence against them was lacking, warned that they were being watched and urged to get out of town.

Violette was only twenty years old when she joined the staff of the Sûreté in 1819 or thereabouts, and she was still a member of the organization eight years later, when Vidocq retired for the first time. He wrote that she performed valuable services and was directly responsible for the arrest and imprisonment of "more than a score" of criminals.

The motives that prompted a woman in Violette's profession to act as a police agent can only be guessed. Little is known about Vidocq's pay scale, but it is doubtful that she earned as much as an informer as she did entertaining a client in her primary profession. Perhaps she was bored by her own work and enjoyed the excitement of being instrumental in sending criminals to prison.

Greed was the reason Maude Leclerc worked for the Sûreté, and she made no secret of it. Eventually achieving a considerable notoriety in her own right, she was one of the few women employed by Vidocq whose full identity was known.

As a slum streetwalker in her early teens, she became the mistress of a man sent to the guillotine for murder, and thereafter, in succession, she lived with three others who served long prison terms for robbery. Tough and resilient, she continued to ply her trade and, by the time she reached her early twenties, she owned her own brothel in the rough Marais district of Paris.

Criminals on the run from the authorities sometimes found refuge under her roof, and as Vidocq knew from his own experience, there was no safer overnight hiding place than the bed of a prostitute. He made a private deal with Maude Leclerc, arranging for her to use her younger brother and sister as secret messengers when an escaped convict or a criminal in hiding spent the night with one of her girls.

If her connection with the Sûreté had become known, it is likely that one of her guests would have slit her throat. So Vidocq made certain that no arrests were made at Maude's brothel. Sometimes his detectives came to the establishment and spent the night in rooms adjoining that of the fleeing criminal and picked him up the next day after he had left the place. On other occasions they kept watch from a room rented for the purpose across the street. None of the men apprehended after finding refuge under her roof ever knew that she had played a key role in his arrest.

Maude Leclerc remained on the staff of the Sûreté for almost twenty years, staying on after Vidocq's final departure. During that time, or so she informed Dumas, she was directly responsible for the capture of more than fifty criminals. By the time she revealed her story she had moved to a middle-class neighborhood, where she lived in comfort under a new name. Like so many Sûreté alumni, she continued to think of Vidocq as the greatest man she had ever known.

Many of the criminals whom he sent to prison also regarded him with a mixture of awe and superstitious wonder, and without realizing what they were doing, contributed to the legend of his invincibility. His fame spread from the Paris underworld to the nether regions of other major European cities long before respectable citizens knew of his existence and learned of his accomplishments.

In 1833 Dumas wrote a newspaper article, later reprinted in several magazines, in which Vidocq was portrayed as an intrepid mastermind. He needed only to appear in the haunts of criminals, announce, "I am Vidocq!" for men wanted by the authorities for a variety of crimes to give themselves up; he had then only to quietly accept their surrender. The story was an exaggeration but did contain an element of truth. By 1820, eight years after the founding of the Brigade de la Sûreté, the crime rate of Paris had been reduced by an astonishing 40 per cent, and the Sûreté was responsible for most of the credit. The criminals had good reason to believe their nemesis was endowed with almost supernatural wisdom and strength.

Within two years of the Bourbon restoration Vidocq was a man of consequence in France. The remarkable success of the Sûreté guaranteed its survival and continuing growth, his moneylending earned him a large income and the prospects of his special paper and ink manufacture were bright. He had moved his mother to a large town house near the Palais Royal, where she was attended by a cook and housemaid, and when she went out she rode in his comfortable carriage.

But a heavy cloud continued to hang over his head. He was still an escaped convict and, technically, could be returned to the galleys to serve the rest of his uncompleted prison term. He would be truly free only when he received a royal pardon for the forgery he had committed in his youth. His future was insecure, the government was embarrassed and the uniformed police often reminded him of his precarious position.

Highly placed friends were determined to have him restored to full citizenship. Perhaps the most important of them was a former superior and a fellow holdover from the Empire, Baron Charles de Pasquier. At one time the Prefect of the Paris police, he was now Minister of Justice and was more advantageously placed than anyone else to aid his former subordinate.

In March, 1817, Pasquier prepared a pardon, which Louis XVIII signed on April 12th. Under the law Vidocq was required to appear in person before the court in Douai, where the original sentence had been passed, but Pasquier spared him even this minor mortification by sending a copy of the pardon to Douai with a letter explaining that Vidocq's work for the government was of such a confidential nature that his appearance would have been injurious to the security of the state.

On May 2, 1817, Vidocq received a formal letter from the President of the Douai court informing him that the forgery charge against him had been expunged from the record. He was no longer a fugitive, he could vote and had the right to carry a passport that would enable him to travel abroad. What really mattered was that there was no way his enemies could conspire to send him back to prison.

Free at last, Vidocq celebrated by giving a dinner party at one of the most fashionable restaurants in Paris, and his guests included Pasquier and three of the highest-ranking officials of the uniformed police. No wives were present; instead Vidocq thoughtfully provided his guests with the company of several of the loveliest courtesans in the city.

In 1820 Vidocq married for the second time. He was forty-five and his bride, Jeanne-Victoire Guerin, was twenty-one. Little is known about her other than that she was exceptionally beautiful and brought no dowry with her. Her actual identity has been the subject of romantic speculation for more than a century and a half.

Articles in the press inspired by Vidocq's foes in the 1830's and 1840's indicated that he had advertised for her in the personal columns of the newspapers and that he had married her for her money, but these claims are palpably false. Attractive women surrounded Vidocq, and there was no need for him to advertise for a bride. The Bureau of Registry, where all marriages in Paris were recorded, still has on file the yellowing pages of the marriage application that prove it was Vidocq, not his wife, who had the money. He swore that he had 80,000 francs in cash and securities, as well as property worth another 32,000 francs. Jeanne-Victoire had nothing.

Vidocq never mentioned this brief, tragic marriage to Victor Hugo, Honoré de Balzac or any of his other literary friends, and he cut them off on the few occasions when they brought up the subject. Naturally they wondered about her.

Balzac was certain that she had been a courtesan, and that Vidocq married her after falling in love with her in order to remove her from a distasteful profession. Hugo's account is more richly romantic. Jeanne-Victoire, he believed, was a country girl who came to Paris and fell in with criminals. Vidocq, after falling in love with her, married her to prevent her from committing a misdeed that would send her to prison.

Whoever she may have been, her new husband proudly moved her into the large new house he had just purchased on the rue de l'Hirondelle, where his mother occupied her own suite. For the next year and a half he dined in public frequently with his new wife, and sometimes his mother accompanied them. It may be too much to expect that he gave up his models, actresses and courtesans, but he no longer paraded them before his friends and acquaintances.

In the autumn of 1822 he resumed his old ways, escorting the light ladies of the town, and skeptics snickered. What neither they nor anyone else knew was that the new Mme. Vidocq had fallen ill of a disease then known as an "impaired heart" and later called rheumatic fever. She was badly crippled, confined to her bed, and there was nothing the physicians could do to help her.

Jeanne-Victoire died on September 23, 1824. One month later, to the day, Vidocq's mother expired.

He was urged to take a leave of absence and travel abroad until he recovered from his double tragedy, but he refused the suggestion, supposedly saying, "The underworld never rests, so I cannot afford a holiday." He took refuge in his work, going home infrequently and, more often than not, snatching a few hours of sleep on a cot in his office. Twelve years after first setting up the Brigade de la Sûreté in 1812, the forty-nine-year-old Vidocq reverted to the schedules of the bureau's earliest days. No longer dining in public, he snatched meals at headquarters with his men. He had no time for women, rarely saw his friends and, for the next year, worked almost without respite. In that year the Sûreté was responsible for 1700 arrests and convictions, and Vidocq personally took credit for three hundred twenty-five, an average of almost one per day. His energy and devotion to duty further contributed to his legend.

Late in the 1820's he married for the third time; the exact date is unknown because the wedding took place in Arras, and the records no longer exist. His bride was Fleuride Maniez, his cousin, who was the daughter of his mother's sister. He was in his fifties and she was not yet twenty. It is almost needless to add that she was very pretty.

This marriage was completely successful and lasted for more than twenty years. Fleuride appears to have been the perfect wife. She was loving, faithful and loyal, giving him her unstinting support in private and in public when his enemies tried to ruin him and almost succeeded. She was an impeccable housekeeper and was such a shrewd businesswoman that he was able to leave the management of his finances in her hands for long periods. Obviously he trusted her implicitly.

The authors who were his friends from the 1820's until the end of his life in 1857 commented that he often talked about his wife, frequently bought her expensive gifts and plainly was very much in love with her. But it would have been too much to expect him to give up his habits of a lifetime even for such a paragon.

Twice each week Fleuride accompanied her husband to the most fashionable restaurants in Paris, often going on to the theater with him. On other evenings, however, he appeared in the same restaurants with his usual assortment of loose ladies.

What Mme. Vidocq thought of his philandering is not known, but his affairs were so blatant that everyone else in Paris was aware of them, so it is unlikely that she was kept in ignorance. Perhaps she was that rare woman, the understanding wife who knew her husband strayed and who accepted his casual affairs because she realized they meant nothing of consequence to him. Whether she actually condoned his extramarital relationships is impossible to determine, but the facts speak for themselves: Vidocq and Fleuride stayed married and lived together until her death, and he continued to engage in his endless round of affairs.

Certainly his life changed after his marriage to Fleuride Maniez. He adopted disguises less frequently, took fewer personal risks and devoted more of his time to supervising the work of his subordinates rather than handling dangerous cases himself. He gained weight for the first time, and although he continued to wear expensive clothes his attire became less flamboyant.

His marriage may have been partly responsible for his more sedate attitudes, but other factors were at work, too, chief among them being the place he held in Paris officialdom. Ever since Napoleon Bonaparte had made himself First Consul before the turn of the century, it had been customary for only one police official, the Prefect himself, to associate with the magistrates. Lesser officials, including the Deputy Prefects, channeled all of their business through the one man at the top.

It is true that the Brigade de la Sûreté was something of a separate branch since it operated apart from the uniformed police, but it nevertheless was a branch, and Vidocq held the rank of a Deputy Prefect. The unique regard in which it was held was a tribute to its founder, and in the Sûreté of the period could be seen the seeds of the even more extraordinary organization it would later become.

As the world's first detective police force using specially trained men in civilian clothes to solve crimes scientifically, the Brigade de la Sûreté was the prototype for Scotland Yard and the Federal Bureau of Investigation. That it was the pioneer is noteworthy; that it was entirely the product of one man's vision, skill and ingenuity is remarkable.

Vidocq had no precedents to guide him and had to feel his way, frequently fighting the jealous uniformed police hierarchy. Even in his own day, however, the courts appreciated his efforts. Today thousands of detective departments and bureaus everywhere on earth are in his debt, and the Sûreté of the late twentieth century remains a model of efficiency.

It was typical of Vidocq that he chose to ignore tradition and established his own relations with the magistrates, a practice the Sûreté has followed for a century and a half. The bureau in its official capacity investigated crimes and brought their perpetrators to justice; its chief informally assumed additional functions as a special prosecutor and friend of the courts.

Such duties would not be permitted in the United States, Great Britain or other English-speaking countries because they are opposed to the basic Anglo-Saxon concept of justice. But they fit nicely within the overall framework of the Code Napoleon, and it is not accidental that the head of today's Sûreté maintains the traditions so blithely established by Vidocq.

By the mid-1820's his personal relations with many of the magistrates were so solid that he not only visited them privately in their chambers but frequently was seen dining with them. It appears that he alone among police officials was their social equal. Not even the Prefect dared to presume on his acquaintance with them to this extent, and the commissaires had another grudge to chalk up against Vidocq. It was inconceivable to them that a former convict and former fugitive from justice should be on close terms with the august members of the bench. Under the Code Napoleon a presiding magistrate had — and still has — great independent powers, and they resented Vidocq's easy familiarity with the judges.

Not that their opposition bothered him or caused him to mend his ways. On the contrary, he did what he thought best for the Sûreté and himself. He ignored his critics and did not bother to reply to them. Had he wished he could have fought them within the Prefecture, using his influence with the courts as a weapon, or he could have taken his counter-complaints to the press. He was already a favorite of the newspapers, although he shrouded his activities in mystery, and the reporters would have been happy to give his views a full hearing. He chose to do neither, strictly minded his own business and let the records being amassed by the Sûreté speak for themselves.

It is strange that this combative, egocentric and ambitious

man should have adopted such a passive attitude toward jealous colleagues who sniped at him so incessantly, lost no opportunity to ridicule his operations and denigrated him personally. Perhaps his seeming indifference was intended as a sign of his contempt for gadflies he regarded as harmless.

As a student of human nature he should have known better. His enemies in the Prefecture interpreted his refusal to strike back as a sign of weakness, and their determination to cripple him became greater. Vidocq was storing up serious trouble for himself, and one day there would be an explosion.

VIII

VIDOCQ'S PERSONALITY was compelling and the favorable publicity he received in print was so great that his contemporaries held him solely responsible for the success of the Sûreté Nationale. This was a warped, highly prejudiced view; the Sûreté was no more a one-man show than was the FBI of J. Edgar Hoover's era.

Vidocq was aided by a number of exceptionally competent assistants, as well as by others whose rogue spots remained unchanged. Certainly he deserves full credit for the judgment that enabled him to select and train so many first-rate detectives.

Heading the list was André Goury, a one-time swindler who became the assistant chief of the Sûreté, learned Vidocq's methods and applied them with vigor. Tall, somewhat ungainly and perennially cheerful, Goury was a perfect foil for his superior, following his orders to the letter and taking his own initiatives in ways he knew Vidocq would approve of. He was fanatically loyal, never forgetting that it had been Vidocq who had given him the opportunity to rehabilitate himself, and whenever he was in charge of the bureau, he always issued commands in his superior's name.

Goury was endowed with Vidocq's understanding of the criminal mentality, which he had acquired in part from his own experience and partly through long discussions with the head of the Sûreté. He lacked, however, Vidocq's instinctive grasp of what a criminal might do in any given situation, but there were not many who had that quality. It was Vidocq's hope, as well as his own, that he would eventually take the top place at the Sûreté, but the post was denied him because he had never been pardoned for the two prison terms he had served.

There was a rough element in both men that the authors who wrote about Vidocq failed to see. It is best illustrated, perhaps, by an incident that occurred in the mid-1820's. For many years Goury had lived with a handsome woman named Marie, and he eventually married her. One evening, before their marriage, she walked to Vidocq's house, intending to join him and her lover for dinner, and was followed by a well-dressed, middle-aged man who mistakenly thought she was a prostitute.

When she explained what had happened to Goury and Vidocq they promptly admitted the man to the house and conducted him to a dark upstairs bedroom. There he was joined by a woman he believed to be the one he had followed. Not until too late did he discover she was an elderly, ugly maid of all work. Even then he was locked in with her for the night and was not permitted to leave the next morning until he had paid a large fee, which Goury and Vidocq gave to the crone. Obviously the pair had their own sense of justice.

Third in command of the Sûreté was a man named Charles Fouché, who was not related to Napoleon's Minister of the Police and Interior, Joseph Fouché. A bull-like, athletic man, Fouché had been imprisoned at sixteen for armed robbery, and had gone to work for the Sûreté eight years later, immediately after his release. He acquired Vidocq's ability to wear disguises, at least to some extent, but he was valuable principally because of his raw courage.

When Vidocq didn't lead a raid in person, that task was given to Fouché, particularly when it was believed that the criminals involved would put up a struggle. On one occasion, when rounding up a gang of robbers who had committed a number of murders, Fouché and two associates succeeded in subduing no fewer than nine men after a bloody fight.

On another occasion, when Vidocq asked for uniformed police to assist in a raid, he was told by the Deputy Prefect in charge of the division that he was asking for the impossible. A full regiment would be needed for the task.

Vidocq replied that he and Fouché could and would perform the duty without any help, and this they did, taking twenty-one hardened criminals into custody and marching them to the nearest police station. They accomplished the feat by assaulting the two leaders of the gang, pummeling them so severely that the others meekly surrendered.

Of all the detectives employed by the Sûreté, Vidocq's personal favorite was a charming scoundrel from Naples named Ronquetti. He first appeared in Paris in the winter of 1816–1817, accompanied by a beautiful Italian mistress, and, calling himself the Duke of Modena, rented an expensive apartment in the vicinity of the Palais Royal.

He spent his afternoons and evenings at the gaming houses, where he won consistently at cards, and these facts were duly reported to the Sûreté by agents who kept watch on gambling establishments and were suspicious of newcomers. Even during the early years of the bureau Vidocq assigned specialists to his sub-departments, a policy that paid off repeatedly.

Ronquetti was so clever that the gambling experts were unable to catch him cheating at cards, but he never lost, and Vidocq had him brought to his headquarters for a chat. Ronquetti readily admitted his real identity, even though no charges were brought against him, and immediately accepted an offer to go to work for the Sûreté.

By the following year he was in charge of the gambling squad, still maintaining his public pose as the Duke of Modena, and he kept the position for the next twenty-five years. During that time he was responsible for the arrest and conviction of scores of card sharks, and it was said he was familiar with every trick they might play.

In the late spring of 1819, Ronquetti repaid his debt to the man who had saved him from eventual exposure and imprisonment. Vidocq walked home from his headquarters late one night, wanting exercise and fresh air, and had no idea that a gang of thieves was lying in wait for him near his house, intending to kill him.

Ronquetti happened to be passing in the opposite direction, saw the gang and guessed their intentions. Soon he encountered Vidocq, to whom he told his suspicions, and together they subdued and arrested the would-be killers, Ronquetti proving as expert with pistol and sword as he was with a deck of cards.

A one-time forger named Aubé served for many years as general secretary of the Sûreté. He was given the position as the result of an incident in which he earned Vidocq's complete trust.

Vidocq's budget was secret, and at his insistence the Sûreté's funds for salaries, expenses and agents' rewards were paid to him in cash on the last day of each month by the Ministry of Finance. One day in 1820 he stopped at his office en route to the bank after collecting the Sûreté funds at the Ministry, and without realizing it, dropped a large stack of money on the floor of his anteroom. He then left for the bank.

Aubé, who happened to pass him in the corridor, saw the pile of banknotes on the floor, closed the door and refused to let anyone enter the Chief's suite. Meanwhile Vidocq made his deposit, still unaware of what had happened, and when he returned to his office Aubé pointed at the thick roll of bills on the floor.

As Vidocq well knew, a dozen of the former criminals on his staff would have committed murder for that much money. Aubé refused a generous reward, saying he would accept only a glass of wine, and that the honor was worth 10,000 francs. That same day he became a member of Vidocq's personal staff and, within a short time, he knew all of the Sûreté's many secrets. He never betrayed his trust, and thirty-seven years later he served as one of Vidocq's pallbearers.

Not all of the agents Vidocq employed deserved his confidence, and occasionally one tried to betray him. Only his own vigilance saved him from the treachery of a petty thief named Manceau, a youth still in his teens whom Vidocq tried to rehabilitate. Captured after committing several burglaries, Manceau was offered a choice: he could either work for the Sûreté or go to prison. Naturally he chose the more attractive alternative.

Most newcomers to the bureau served a year's probation, performing minor functions until they could be trusted. Manceau belonged in this category and for six months he made no mistakes. Then he slipped.

One day he was ordered to conduct a disguised Vidocq to a slum tavern where several criminals wanted by the authorities for major crimes were scheduled to hold a meeting. While walking to the rendezvous with his courier Vidocq observed that his behavior was odd. Manceau replied in vague monosyllables to remarks addressed to him and refused to meet his eye.

Aware that something out of the ordinary was taking place, Vidocq questioned him closely and learned that Manceau had revealed his true identity to the woman who owned the tavern, and that the murderers who were meeting there intended to kill him. He summoned reinforcements, but the criminals were alarmed by the fact that he did not arrive alone and fled. They were not captured until several months later.

Vidocq could be ruthless when the occasion warranted, and young Manceau paid for his perfidy. The charges against him were reinstituted without delay, and he was sentenced to a six-year prison term. He tried to escape, was sent to the galleys and died after being subjected to brutal treatment there.

The employee who created the most troubles for Vidocq was the clever, effeminate Coco Lacour, who had started his criminal career as a procurer for a brothel at the age of eleven. In 1810 when Vidocq worked as a police informer, his testimony sent Coco to prison for two years, but in 1813, a year after the Brigade de la Sûreté was founded, Vidocq hired the recently released youth, whose intelligence and wit had impressed him.

Coco, who never forgave him, bided his time and waited until 1817, when he had achieved the rank of a senior agent. A number of detectives were chronically unhappy, believing that the rewards they were given were too small, and Coco encouraged their discontent by telling them that Vidocq was privately pocketing funds he should have passed along to them.

Late in 1817 three agents wrote a letter to the President of the Examining Court, charging Vidocq with accepting bribes. One said he had paid the Chief of the Sûreté two hundred francs to have a sentence reduced, while another said he had been given a position in the bureau in return for his silence regarding blackmail that Vidocq supposedly had perpetrated.

The charges were so serious that the public prosecutor was required to make a thorough investigation, but no positive evidence against Vidocq was found. The agents responsible for the mischief changed their stories and said they had been urged by Coco Lacour to create trouble.

The allegations could not be proved, and Coco defended himself with such agility that Vidocq believed him and kept him on the job. Perhaps the greatest weakness that Vidocq repeatedly demonstrated was that of accepting the veracity of former criminals. He was convinced that every convict would mend his ways if given the opportunity and he took Coco at his word. In time he would regret his generosity.

Remarkably few of the former criminals Vidocq hired caused problems for him, however, and each year his position became more secure. One important but hidden source of his growing strength lay in his relations with the people he called his "good neighbors of the faubourg Saint-Germain," the dukes, counts and barons of both the Bourbon aristocracy and the upstarts whom Napoleon had ennobled.

Many of these powerful, wealthy lords and their pampered ladies had more money than common sense. They committed sexual and social indiscretions and indulged in excesses because they considered themselves beyond the reach of the law. They then discovered that they were on the brink of a scandal or about to be hauled into court for committing crimes and that they desperately needed immediate help.

For example, there was Comte X, a slender and personable young man of great wealth who, to relieve his boredom, dressed in women's attire and stole the jewelry of his friends' wives. Another was the daughter of a duke who collected thousands of francs each year by blackmailing her uncle, a distinguished gentleman and high-ranking government official, whom she had discovered to have a homosexual liaison.

More than anyone else in Paris Vidocq was in a position to help these wealthy unfortunates, and they and their relatives flocked to him. A duke who wanted concrete evidence that his wife was being unfaithful knew where to go to obtain the facts. A baron afraid that his son was being used by confidence men knew who could break up the relationship.

Vidocq was always discreet and glad to be of assistance. For years he denied that he ever accepted gifts in return for the favors he did the people of wealth and power, but as an old man he finally broke down and admitted that it would have been rude and ungracious to refuse new furniture for his country house, a team of matched horses to pull his carriage or a pair of diamond earrings for his wife. Never, he insisted, had he taken cash for his services, as that would have been a form of bribery.

By 1820 or thereabouts, he was a familiar figure in the faubourg Saint-Germain. Unless he was engaged in official business on behalf of the Sûreté he did not receive a visitor at his office, but instead went to the troubled aristocrat's home for a cup of tea or glass of wine.

His attitude on these occasions was a curious blend of arrogance and humility. He made no guarantees but promised results and more often than not he solved the problem. Yet he never presumed on the relationships he established. When dining at his favorite restaurant in the Place du Châtelet, one of the city's most fashionable establishments, he never spoke to a duke or countess unless he was addressed first. If they chose to keep silent about the services he was rendering them, that was their privilege.

It was these hidden friendships that kept Vidocq afloat in the treacherous sea of French politics for so many years. He was not important enough to be dismissed when Napoleon went into exile, and the Bourbon restoration was established on firm ground. He not only survived the Revolutions of 1830 and 1848, but he rendered valuable services to several factions. He was friendly with Louis Napoleon before that questionable worthy became President of France and then established the Second Empire. Regarding politics as a boring game unworthy of his talents, he concentrated on the building of his own, highly specialized power base and cultivated fame and fortune with remarkable results.

By the time of the Revolution of 1830, to use the language of a later era, he knew where too many bodies were buried for anyone to neglect or to try to harm him. He had become the confidant of everyone of consequence who had something to hide.

His energy was inexhaustible because he loved his work and he loved money. By the mid-1820's the Brigade de la Sûreté had a staff of more than one hundred twenty persons, and there was no need for Vidocq to investigate cases in person. But he deliberately chose to climb into various disguises several days each week. One day he was a general, the next a foreign merchant, the third a pickpocket. The first time Balzac went to his home Vidocq took him to a secluded room on the top floor, carefully unlocked a door and showed his astonished visitor row after row of costumes, box after box of wigs, mustaches and beards. Vidocq was a natural actor who relished playing his various roles on a stage that included all France.

He was a wealthy man now, worth perhaps as much as 500,000 francs. His enemies insisted he acquired most of it by illegal means, but they were mistaken. He took care never to break the law. Moneylending was legal, and if he chose to accept an expensive gift from a rich friend that was his private affair. Sometimes, too, he listened to suggestions from people he had helped. He was told to buy properties in various neighborhoods and, after doing so, within months sold them at a profit. When it was hinted that he purchase stock in a company he acted accordingly, and was duly delighted when new owners bought it soon thereafter, doubling his money.

Grateful to his benefactors, Vidocq helped them in return. When a disgruntled mistress threatened to cause problems for a gentleman unless he paid her large sums of money, the Chief of the Sûreté paid a private call on her, and she hastily departed for foreign parts. When the son of a noble family fell in with thieves he was summoned to Vidocq's office for a chat and usually went off for a long holiday in Switzerland or the Italian states, with no formal charges being made against him.

Although Vidocq did not advertise his friendships with the prominent and influential, he made no secret of them either. He and his contemporaries found nothing immoral in his favor-exchanging relationships, and there was no precedent to guide him. He lived in a pragmatic world.

Not even the wealthy could escape the consequences of committing a major crime, however. Vidocq tracked down murderers of every class, and a robber was sent to prison no matter how blue his blood. If an aristocratic burglar made full restitution to his victims Vidocq might be persuaded to look the other way, but if the crime was repeated he pursued the perpetrator until he was caught, charged and brought to justice.

The basic source of his strength, as rich and poor alike realized, was his knowledge of the criminal mind. His own long years in the underworld had given him unmatched opportunities to study outlaws of every kind, and he apparently forgot nothing he had ever heard or seen.

One night in the mid-1830's Vidocq was persuaded, when dining with Victor Hugo at the Grand Vefour Restaurant near the Palais Royal, to talk about the superstitions that influenced lawbreakers and he delivered a monologue that lasted for the better part of the night. The Sûreté and the uniformed police had less to do on Fridays than on any other day of the week, Vidocq said, because no criminal ever initiated a major enterprise on Fridays. If the first person passed on the street when a criminal went off to do a job was a priest, the project was postponed for at least twenty-four hours. This rule was observed by Protestants, Jews and atheists as well as by Catholics.

If the first person seen abroad at the beginning of a work day was a nun, the job had to be put off for a week even if the criminal starved during that time. If he saw and retrieved a piece of iron — ranging in size from a tiny fleck to a large crowbar — his enterprise could not fail. When a murder was planned, the killer had to sleep the previous night with some woman other than his wife or regular mistress, but he could go to bed only with his accustomed mate the night before perpetrating a major robbery.

Under no circumstances could a man allow his hat to rest on a bed. If this happened he was sure to be picked up by the police within the next twenty-four hours. This catastrophe could be averted only if he deflowered a virgin, provided she was not related to him by blood or marriage. A swindler drank no wine for three hours before fleecing a victim, and a wise burglar always drank a glass of caraway-flavored water before going to work.

In spite of Vidocq's knowledge of the criminal's beliefs and familiarity with his haunts, he was sometimes hampered by forces seemingly beyond his control. In 1824, after the death of the mild, ineffectual Louis XVIII, the ultra-reactionary Charles X ascended the throne. Convinced that Napoleon's devoted followers intended to restore his line, the new monarch ordered the police to devote their time and efforts to finding these traitors, obtaining evidence that they were plotting against the crown and sending them to prison.

A new Prefect of police was appointed, and Guy Delaveau was even more zealous than King Charles X. Police were taken off crime beats to search the newspapers for seditious material and to attend plays to make certain there was no gesture on the Paris stage that might be interpreted as a slap at Bourbon majesty. Delaveau found Bonapartists everywhere, and the rate of robberies, burglaries and other crimes in the city increased.

The Brigade de la Sûreté was ordered to search for traitors, too, but Vidocq paid no attention to the instructions. At no previous time had he participated in political activities and he had no intention of allowing the bureau to become involved now. He filed his new orders and continued to hunt criminals.

Although Delaveau was obsessed by Bonapartists he was a pleasure-loving man, married to a much younger wife, and he paid little attention to business. Most of the work of the Prefecture was supervised by his secretary, Marc Duplessis, an ambitious young man of twenty-two who was given a Spanish medal as a courtesy and thereafter insisted on being addressed as "Chevalier" Duplessis.

Vidocq happily ignored Delaveau and his secretary and

went about his own business until the night, late in 1825, when Mme. Delaveau left her cape in her carriage while attending the theater and, when sending for it, discovered it had been stolen. Her husband, by this time convinced of his own importance, sent for the Deputy Prefect in charge of the Sûreté and ordered him to find the cape.

Vidocq thought he was joking, but when Delaveau angrily repeated the command, ten detectives were assigned to the case. By the time the performance at the theater came to an end, Vidocq had returned and placed her recovered cape around the lady's shoulders.

The Prefect didn't like his Deputy's attitude, regarding him as insolent, and this soon translated itself into the thought that he might be a Bonapartist. Delaveau ordered his secretary to keep watch on the Chief of the Sûreté.

Nothing could have pleased Duplessis more. Vidocq habitually treated him like a child, refused to address him as "Chevalier" and wouldn't listen to suggestions that would have "improved" the performance of the bureau.

Duplessis assigned men from the Prefect's office to spy on the Brigade de la Sûreté, but the agents quickly learned of these bumbling efforts and first shrugged them off, then played deliberate, insulting tricks on the amateurs.

Unable to find any evidence of treason in the Sûreté, Duplessis found release for his frustration in a memorandum he sent to Vidocq in October, 1826. In it he sharply criticized Sûreté employees for their off-duty conduct, saying that many of the agents visited brothels and drank in public places.

Vidocq thought the secretary was merely inexperienced and replied in a humorous vein, saying that he himself was rarely abstemious at dinner and that he was a friend of the inmates of several fashionable brothels. Then he put the matter out of his mind.

Duplessis was not content to let the matter rest and, in

mid-June, 1827, he wrote again to Vidocq, saying that several agents had become intoxicated at a café after work the previous night, and insisted that they be dismissed from the service without delay.

"Apart from the fact that this young man did not share my opinions," Vidocq later remarked, "he had manners which were not to my liking and a way of giving orders which I could not accept." So, on June 20, 1827, the Chief of the Sûreté submitted his resignation in a letter that said:

> For eighteen years I have served the police with distinction. I have never received a single reproach from your predecessors; I must therefore think that I have never deserved one. Since your nomination to the Prefecture this is the second time you have done me the honor to address one to me in complaining of the agents.
>
> Am I their master in their spare time? No.
>
> To save you, Monsieur, the inconvenience of addressing me any similar complaints in future, and myself the trouble of receiving them, I have the honor to ask you to be good enough to accept my resignation without delay.

Chevalier Duplessis accepted the resignation that same day on behalf of Prefect Delaveau, and Vidocq's enemies in the uniformed police rejoiced, but their pleasure was mild compared to the delight of the underworld.

IX

VIDOCQ'S RESIGNATION from the Sûreté caused a sensation, but the bureau itself was so solidly established that no one even thought of dissolving it. Chevalier Duplessis, who was the proud possessor of a sure instinct for the absurd, appointed Coco Lacour as the great detective's successor, and the underworld snickered. Henceforth criminals who had been harassed and hounded would be free to do as they pleased, and the rate of robberies, burglaries and purse-snatchings rose overnight.

Late in August Vidocq was in the news again, the Paris press reporting in bold type that he had been hanged in Vienna after making an unsuccessful attempt to assassinate Napoleon's son, the Duke of Reichstadt, who had been living at the Austrian court in semi-confinement. No motive was given for the act.

Newspapers from Moscow to New York reprinted the story, which continued to create such a stir that on August 28th, simultaneous announcements were made by the Ministry of Justice in Paris and the Chamberlain of the Imperial court in Vienna: the claim had no basis in fact.

As it happened, Vidocq was very much alive, enjoying the best of health and settling into a small country estate he and his wife had bought outside the village of Saint-Mandé, near Vincennes, about an hour's drive from Paris. The main house was modest for a man of means. Made of stone, it had a salon, library, dining room and kitchen on the ground floor, five bedrooms on the second floor and, on the third, an attic that Vidocq converted into a laboratory. His wife had a vegetable garden large enough to supply friends with produce, and the orchard, consisting of ten acres of fruit trees, required the full-time services of a gardener.

Vidocq's enemies claimed that the stones used to build the house had been removed from the Seine by Sûreté detectives during working hours, and the story was widely believed. Vidocq, who was now fifty-two years old and resting for the first time in his active life, did not bother to point out that the place had been standing for many years before he had purchased it.

Soon after his retirement, one of his many money-making ventures came to light. He was engaged in the business of finding substitutes for men called to serve in the army, charging a flat fee and giving a portion of the bonus to those who took the places of conscripts. Any number of people were engaged in similar enterprises, which were legitimate and lawful. It was claimed that Vidocq provided criminals for the purpose, and that men who otherwise would have been sent to prison were delighted to escape into uniform. Vidocq ignored the charges, which well may have been true.

At about the same time it was also revealed that he was the proprietor of five taverns located in the same working-class district, three in the rue de la Juiverie and the others nearby, behind the Place de la Grève. He made no secret of these holdings, telling Hugo that he had opened the first of them in 1813 and had put Annette in charge when she had retired as his unofficial assistant at the Sûreté. He also admitted that he himself had sometimes worked in these establishments, disguised as a bartender or waiter.

Vidocq offered no reason for this curious behavior, but his motives were obvious. His taverns were frequented by thieves and prostitutes who long had realized what the law-abiding citizens of Paris had not known, that Vidocq owned these places. They believed they could drink there with impunity because the head of the Sûreté would not have ordered raids on his own properties.

What they failed to realize was that a disguised Sûreté agent was always on duty at each tavern, and sent in daily reports on conversations of consequence that he had overheard. So Vidocq not only made a profit on his taverns but was provided with important, convenient sources of information regarding criminal activities at the same time.

He continued to own and operate these drinking places after his retirement from the Sûreté, and they remained immune from raids, even though most of their customers were members of the underworld. Coco Lacour would have enjoyed hitting his former superior in the pocketbook, but refrained, so it can only be guessed that Vidocq continued to supply the Sûreté with information in return for the right to serve dubious patrons without interference.

Almost immediately after his retirement, Vidocq expanded his moneylending activities and added a new line to that business — the collection of debts owed to others. This operation was supervised by a burly former bailiff named Pepin, who was assisted by several ex-agents of the Sûreté, men still loyal to Vidocq whom Lacour had dismissed. It may be guessed that these retired detectives, themselves one-time criminals, found ways to bully debtors into paying claims they owed.

Vidocq's grand enterprise, which he launched within a short time of his retirement, was the establishment of a paper-box factory at Saint-Mandé, built with funds supplied in part out of his own purse and partly by a wealthy philanthropist, Benjamin Appert. Here Vidocq put one of his pet theories on rehabilitation of criminals into operation: almost without exception his employees — from factory workers to salesmen — were former convicts who could find no other honest work.

The ex-prisoner in the 1820's found it even more difficult

to survive than did his his successors in later generations. He was forbidden to take up residence in Paris or any of the other major cities and, if caught there by the police, was re-arrested and sentenced to another term in jail. Honest people in the smaller communities were reluctant to hire these men, and even those who seriously wanted to reform were driven back almost inevitably into a life of crime.

Vidocq proposed to change all that. He had living quarters constructed near the paper-box factory and sent out word that ex-convicts were welcome. For six months while a man was being trained for his job, he was given food, clothing and shelter; thereafter he was paid a living wage. The door was opened, too, to former women prisoners whose only alternative was a life of prostitution.

The experiment was unique and caused a storm of interest, reactionaries decrying and liberals praising it. Eugène Sue, who was just beginning his writing career after working as a naval surgeon, and who later became an active socialist, was fascinated and subsequently admitted his debt to Vidocq in first arousing his interest in criminal rehabilitation.

Illiterates made and dried the cardboard, then fashioned it into boxes. Forgers and other educated men acted as supervisors, and personable swindlers were trained as salesmen. Even the managers of the enterprise were former convicts, and Vidocq himself acted only as an overall supervisor, interfering as little as possible with the daily activities.

Writing about the experiment in later years, he said:

> I employed men who had only known one trade in their lives, that of the thief; men who had many convictions, who might be said to be incorrigible. Yet I never had cause to complain of them.
>
> I can stand up and say that not one of the ex-prisoners to whom I gave work broke faith with me while he was in my employ. It is true, to be sure, that some were dismissed, either for drunkenness or incapacity, and were returned to the surveillance of the provincial police. Then, and only then, they got themselves convicted again.

I repeat, for I am within myself totally convinced of it, that the great majority of ex-prisoners can be reformed. But the decent elements of society must assist and take part in this reformation. The man or woman must be trusted if he is to mend his ways and must see with his own eyes that honorable people are willing to give him the opportunity to change his spots.

A number of companies that had a need for paper boxes approved of what Vidocq was doing and bought his product, but more were offended. The time was not yet ripe for the experiment, and Vidocq lost considerable sums of money. He persevered, however, siphoning the profits earned by other enterprises into the paper-box factory until the upheavals caused by the Revolution of 1830 forced him to close his doors and sell his factory and dormitory buildings.

The venture was his only failure and nagged at him for the rest of his life. His financial losses were of no importance to him, his other sources of income more than making up for them. What bothered him was that a principle in which he believed passionately had not worked out, and over the next quarter of a century he frequently discussed the project with his friends, always insisting that his basic idea had been valid.

Vidocq was still held in such high regard by his fellow citizens that he continued to represent a threat to Coco Lacour and Chevalier Duplessis, whose crime-fighting efforts were resulting in soaring murder, robbery and burglary statistics. So, when a rumor spread in the spring of 1828 to the effect that the pardon granted to Vidocq had been invalid, he suspected these enemies were responsible for the story.

He could have sued them for slander, which would have been difficult to prove, so he chose a simpler method of refuting the lie. Still on friendly terms with influential Paris magistrates, he arranged through them for a formal ceremony to be held at Douai, at which time he would receive a pardon in person.

July 1, 1828, had to be one of the most important days in

Vidocq's life. His pardon from Louis XVIII had been conditional, so he had lived under a shadow. Now, at long last, his full citizenship would be restored, and he would receive such benefits as the right to vote and the right to obtain a passport for travel abroad. Above all, his name would be cleared.

He and a large party set out from Paris several days prior to the great event and traveled in a caravan of carriages. His wife accompanied him, as he very much wanted her to witness the ceremony. Others in the party included several magistrates, government prosecutors and lawyers.

Members of the press were conspicuously absent. Vidocq's enemies had brought his conviction to light, but he had never openly admitted their charges, and he wanted no publicity now. No members of the Sûreté or the uniformed police were members of the group either.

The ceremony itself was brief and dull. The local magistrate read aloud the certificate of pardon and an auxiliary deed restoring to Vidocq the full rights of a citizen of France. The magistrate duly signed both documents, and the party left the courtroom.

Everyone, including the Douai judge, repaired to a local inn, where Vidocq treated his friends to a banquet that lasted for hours. Vast quantities of food and wine were consumed.

Nothing that Lacour and Duplessis might say now could harm Vidocq.

In the late summer of 1828, the first version of his autobiography — which he called his *Mémoires* — was scheduled to be published by Emil Morice, a prominent bookseller with whom Balzac was friendly. The authors with whom Vidocq dined on his frequent visits to Paris saw the galley proofs and protested, saying that the autobiography was far too short. It synopsized his career in a single, slender volume, its brevity an indication that Vidocq might have written it himself.

This work, unfortunately, was little more than an outline and included none of the case histories that the public loved.

So, at the insistence of Hugo, Dumas and Balzac, Vidocq withdrew the project from Morice. The original manuscript and proofs were lost, and whatever they may have contained that accurately portrayed Vidocq's life vanished too.

Soon the retired head of the Sûreté had a new publisher, L. F. L'Héritier de l'Ain. An opportunist, and himself an author of no distinction, L'Héritier soon printed a four-volume version of the *Mémoires*. For a long time it was believed that he was responsible for the expanded account, but the work was prepared so quickly that several writers must have been involved.

The *Mémoires* were published in December, 1828, and were as lacking in literary merit as they were in substance. The approach was lurid and the style was uneven, which more or less confirms the suspicion that each volume was churned out by a different writer.

The Vidocq *Mémoires* rightly may be called the first detective story. Certainly any relation they bore to fact was coincidental. Purporting to tell the story of Vidocq's life, the work was a colorful adventure tale that strained credulity from beginning to end. No man could have lived such an exciting, ever-active life, no man could have performed so many valorous deeds. No attempt was made to present Vidocq realistically, and no attention was paid to his genuine scientific accomplishments. The *Mémoires* stressed action for its own sake and perpetuated the myth of the great detective's invincibility. Without realizing what they were doing, the anonymous authors were setting a precedent for the countless protagonists of detective fiction who proliferated in the next century.

Those who speculated that Hugo or Balzac might have written portions of the *Mémoires* insulted both authors. In their early years both had turned out potboilers, but in even the worst of their work there were glimmers of quality. Dumas could have been responsible because a number of hack writers were already in his employ, writing under his name, but even this is doubtful. The authors of Vidocq's autobiography earned their anonymity.

The public was hungry for stories about Vidocq, and the *Mémoires* were a sensation, becoming an overnight bestseller. More than 50,000 copies sold in the first year after publication, and the four-volume work remained in print throughout Vidocq's own lifetime, selling steadily.

The autobiography was translated into English and appeared in London in the late spring of 1829; British readers were enchanted and bought copies by the thousands. They were more gullible than their French counterparts, however, perhaps because they were unfamiliar with French customs and mores and were more inclined to accept the story literally.

Even the London critics were deeply impressed. "Vidocq must be considered an Asmodeus as to place and a very Proteus as to person," said the learned *Times* reviewer. "Napoleon and Vidocq must go down to posterity together," declared the *Spectator*.

Late in 1829 a play by an unnamed dramatist called *Vidocq! the French Police Spy* was produced by Robert William Elliston at the Surrey Theatre in London, with one of the reigning stars of the English stage, T. P. Cooke, playing the title role. This blatant melodrama borrowed freely from the autobiography and, cheered by opening night audiences, was a smash hit. It, too, made a major contribution to the Vidocq legend. Another play about him, *The Thief Taker of Paris, or Vidocq*, was presented at the Britannia Theatre in London in December, 1860, three years after his death.

The success of the *Mémoires* was responsible for a tidal wave of other books about Vidocq in 1829 and thereafter. Perhaps the best of these dubious efforts was a *Biography of the Founder of the Sûreté, 1812–1827*, written by someone who called himself G——. It was astonishingly crude, totally lacking in style, but had the merit of being relatively authentic in content. Eugène Sue inclined toward the opinion that it might have been written by Vidocq himself, in reply to the fanciful tales written about him.

In 1830 L'Héritier tried to capitalize on the success of the *Mémoires* by bringing out another biography, written under his own name. Called *The Life and Adventures of Vidocq*, it bore no relation to fact and little to the realities of the Sûreté's fight against crime. Later in the year L'Héritier also published a two-volume *Supplement to the Mémoires*, in which he emphasized Vidocq's running feud with the police. He was so vicious in his attacks on both sides that the Prefecture seized the book, banned it and burned all copies. Only one copy of this worthless work still exists and reposes in the files of the Bibliothèque Nationale in Paris.

Yet another publication was a slender book called *Le Para-voleur* that appeared in Paris in 1830, with Vidocq's name listed in large type as the author. This volume supposedly told male and female country dwellers how to avoid trouble when they came to Paris, but was actually thinly disguised erotica. Vidocq neither wrote it nor knew anything about it prior to its publication and tried to have his name removed from the flyleaf. By the time his case came to court in 1831, however, several editions had sold out, and the publisher quietly vanished with his profits.

A Convict's Memoirs, written by two newspaper reporters and published in 1829, tried to take advantage of the Vidocq fad by presenting him as the nemesis of the protagonist. The uniformed police were portrayed as bumbling, inefficient and corrupt, and there was pressure within the Prefecture for the banning of this book, too. Prefect Delaveau resisted on the grounds that he didn't want to make too much of a martyr of Vidocq, and his view ultimately prevailed.

Le Livre noir, its author unlisted, was a free-wheeling assault on Vidocq, the Sûreté and the uniformed police. It supposedly contained the secret correspondence, reports and orders of the Prefecture but was so absurd that both Vidocq and the commissaires ignored it.

La Police dévoilée could not be ignored. Published in 1830, it alleged to be a factual account of crime within the ranks of the police and it tarred Vidocq and his uniformed colleagues with the same brush of corruption. It, too, was banned and burned, and Chevalier Duplessis, his instincts for the ludicrous undiminished by the passage of time, charged that Vidocq had inspired it. Vidocq promptly sued him, and when Duplessis discovered he could not substantiate his claim, he withdrew it, thereby losing face.

The disregard for facts in these and other books may have confused Vidocq's contemporaries but did add to his stature. Almost no one knew the truth about him, and he was enjoying the publicity so much that he bothered to enlighten only his close friends. He was infuriated, however, by an appendix to the English edition of the *Mémoires* in which the anonymous translator said he had been gambling heavily and, at the time of publication, had been sent to prison when caught cheating at cards. The appendix insisted that Vidocq had an illegitimate son named Julius, also a former convict, and that his father had started the paper-box factory in order to give him employment after his release from prison. Julius allegedly had committed another robbery for which he had been returned to prison, so his father had given up the factory. At least it was true that the factory had been sold and closed.

Vidocq might have paid more attention to the lies told about him had he not been preoccupied during the early months of 1830. It had occurred to him that there was a fortune to be made in a burglarproof door lock, and he was spending hours in his third-floor laboratory inventing one.

The Revolution of 1830 intervened, and for several years he was too busy working for the police. He did complete the lock in 1834, however, patenting it the following year. He leased the rights to manufacture the lock, the ancestor of the modern tumbler, and was paid royalties on each one sold. The invention earned him many thousands of francs as well as the gratitude of its purchasers whose homes became relatively safer.

It is no wonder that Vidocq was forced to abandon his experiments with locks in the spring of 1830. France was in ferment, and his retirement came to an abrupt end.

X

A NEW SPIRIT swept through Europe in 1830. People everywhere had grown tired of the authoritarianism of monarchs
clinging to the principles of absolute rule, and the workingman, spurred by the Industrial Revolution that moved him
from a country farm to a city factory, was demanding recogni-
tion of his economic and social rights. People wanted to rule
themselves under a republican form of government, as the
Americans were doing so successfully on the far side of the
Atlantic, and the virus of freedom grew stronger.

Nowhere was the demand for liberty greater than in
France. The autocratic Charles X, who knew little and remembered less, like all Bourbons, had not only forgotten that
he had been driven into exile during the French Revolution
and its Napoleonic aftermath, but had suffered an even more
severe lapse of memory regarding the fate of his brother,
Louis XVI.

Now, in the spring of 1830, the people of Paris were res-
tive, their mood increasingly ugly, and Charles X was in danger of losing both his throne and his life. He might have
saved himself had he been willing to grant greater personal
freedoms, but he was congenitally stubborn, and his ministers shared his myopia. There were severe repressions, and
the crown had few supporters other than the aristocrats.

The republicans were suffering, too, because they were
poorly organized. Their hero was the aged Marquis de Lafay-

ette, hero of both the American and French Revolutions, who was a symbol of freedom throughout both Europe and the New World. Had Lafayette taken a strong stand he could have made himself President of the Republic of France, but he was old, tired and had no desire either for more glory or more responsibility.

The growing middle class was nervous, sitting on the fence and hoping to preserve the wealth it had accumulated since the Revolution. Its unofficial champion was a Bourbon, Louis-Philippe d'Orléans, who managed to present himself to the people as a sober and industrious moderate. He dressed like a notary in somber, inexpensive suits; he walked through the streets of Paris like any bourgeois, explaining that he believed it ostentatious to ride in a carriage; and he conscientiously wooed men of good faith who wanted to avoid more bloodshed.

Precisely how Vidocq fitted into the situation is unknown, and no one has ever learned whose cause he was serving in the spring of 1830, except that it is safe to say he wanted nothing to do with King Charles's Prefect of police, Delaveau. In later years Vidocq remained silent on the subject of his activities from April through July 1830.

It is certain, however, that he was in harness again. His talents were unique, and every faction would have been delighted to avail itself of his services. It is unlikely that he was in the least concerned about such burning problems of the day as the question of the appointment or election of the members of the upper chamber of the national legislature. Such matters had never interested him.

Like most members of his generation who vividly remembered the upheavals of the French Revolution and who had acquired wealth and standing since that time, he could not have sympathized with the young radicals who wanted to abolish the monarchy. His home in the country, his properties in Paris and his various, profitable businesses would be jeopardized in a new civil war. So by a process of elimination, it can be indicated that he stood, in all probability, with the substantial members of the middle class who sought peaceful reforms and thought they could best be achieved by placing Louis-Philippe on the throne as a constitutional monarch.

Everyone except Charles X realized that serious trouble was brewing, and each day in the spring of 1830 the crowds that roamed through the streets grew larger. Vidocq, for whatever his reasons, was spending most of his time in the city, and on May 10th, he joined a mob of artisans and unemployed youths that appeared to be spoiling for a fight.

Suddenly someone recognized him, shouted his name and made a lunge for him. The young men who made up this crowd were opposed to all authority, the name of Vidocq was synonymous with that of the police, and had he been apprehended he would have been severely beaten or even killed.

Before the throng could react, however, he ducked into the district police headquarters on the rue de la Poterie.

His pursuers were afraid to follow him inside, but the commissaire in charge had too few men on hand to control that large a crowd and, in any event, had no desire to spark a riot. So he suggested that a carriage-for-hire be summoned and that Vidocq depart in it. The risks of attempting such a method of escape were obviously great, and Vidocq demurred.

Instead, he donned some rough clothes belonging to a cleaning man that he found in the police station, darkened his hair with lamp black and, slipping out of a side door, calmly rejoined the throng outside. No one knew him now, and he continued to loiter with the crowd for more than an hour before sauntering off to safety.

On July 28th, street fighting broke out when striking printers set up street barricades and were joined by other workers and students. Troops were called out but many sympathized with the rioters and refused to take action against them. Fighting continued for three days, and Charles X, who had made no preparations for such developments, was fortunate to escape with his life.

The aged Lafayette came to his country's rescue again, calling out the national guard, placing himself at its head and restoring order. He could now have become president of a republic but instead believed the promises of Louis-Philippe that he would establish a truly constitutional monarchy and offered him the crown.

The middle class gained the most from the short-lived Revolution of 1830, and on the surface, at least, there were many changes. The Tricolor of the Revolution was substituted for the white banner of the Bourbons, and Louis-Philippe took the new title of King of the French.

The street fighting began at dawn on July 28th, and someone immediately brought the news to Vidocq at Saint-Mandé. At 7:00 A.M. he ran up a Tricolor on the pole that rose from his roof. The local police ordered him to take it down, but he paid no attention to them and ignored a similar demand from the commandant of the military garrison at Vincennes.

Late that morning he disappeared from the house, presumably in disguise, and went to Paris. There he remained throughout the rioting, and not until later, in 1832, was it revealed that he had resumed his duties as Chief of the Sûreté after the July Revolution.

It appears that he had actually rejoined the police several months earlier. Delaveau had been replaced as Prefect earlier in the year by a professional police officer, a commissaire named Anton de Belleyme, who had promptly cleaned house, dismissing Chevalier Duplessis and Coco Lacour. The temporary command of the Sûreté was given to a high-ranking uniformed official named Hebert, but he was unfamiliar with the operations and needs of a detective bureau, and it was agreed when he took the job that he would not keep it.

The ascension of Louis-Philippe to the throne did not end the unrest, and riots continued to erupt in the poorer districts of Paris during the rest of 1830 and most of 1831. One new Prefect of police after another was appointed, but none seemed able to curb the unrest.

Only an official who called himself Laurent was efficient. Wearing the blouse, trousers and boots of an artisan, he worked out of the Prefecture headquarters and had an uncanny ability to recognize potential trouble spots before new riots developed. Again and again workers and students planned to erect barricades at various street intersections, only to find that heavily armed police and troops had arrived on the scene ahead of them.

Newspapers with republican leanings charged that the man known as Laurent was actually Vidocq. To the end of his days Vidocq never admitted the claim but did not deny it either. He was willing to concede that he made his personal headquarters during this time in a large house on the rue Pavée but he was vague in his descriptions of what he did there.

Police records of the period indicate that he reorganized the Sûreté and directed its operations from the rue Pavée. The continuing unrest had caused an increase in the criminal population of Paris, and the new regime also wanted various men with pronounced republican or Bonapartist sympathies kept under surveillance. Vidocq supervised these activities, for the first time extending his operations to the political sphere. He received no publicity, however, and was not given an official appointment as chief of the bureau.

Early in September, 1831, the exceptionally able Casimir Périer was made Minister of Police and the Interior, and immediately appointed a successful, self-made businessman, Henri-Joseph Gisquet, as the Prefect of Paris police. The revolving door was closed, and the new authorities immediately put their house in order.

Périer interviewed Vidocq, then sent him to Gisquet, who knew him only by reputation. The two middle-aged men achieved an immediate rapport, and on October 2, 1831, Vidocq was given a commission as head of the Brigade de la Sûreté, with the rank of Deputy Prefect. At his own request, however, no public announcement was made for the present. He later explained that he wanted to complete his reorganization of the bureau and round up as many criminals as he could before the underworld learned that he was active again.

A number of agents who had worked for him previously returned to the Sûreté, and were joined by the most efficient recruits Vidocq could find. He had maintained his contacts in the criminal world while out of office and apparently had no difficulty in finding and hiring the men and women he wanted.

On March 24, 1832, he was ready and served notice that Vidocq was back. He had learned that a large band of robbers was setting up its base of operations in the town of Gentilly, on the main highway to Paris, so he quietly brought a number of his agents into the town, augmenting the force with a squad of uniformed police who wore civilian clothes for the occasion. Eight members of the gang of robbers were captured, and two who escaped were picked up later in the day. Subsequently they confessed to more than thirty crimes.

The story was given to the press, and Prefect Gisquet simultaneously had the honor to announce that M. Vidocq had been appointed Chief of the Brigade de la Sûreté Nationale, at an annual salary of 6000 francs. Commissaires and other officials of the uniformed police who had hated Vidocq for years were quick to note that he had received an increase in salary of 1000 francs per year. He was the highest-paid Deputy Prefect, and his income was only a trifle smaller than Gisquet's.

Vidocq kept the building on the rue Pavée, establishing offices and housing most of his agents there. But he preferred a less conspicuous base of operations, so he set up his own headquarters in the quiet house on the rue Sainte-Anne that he had used previously. His immediate staff of twenty-eight, which included his assistants, agents and clerks, accompanied him. Minister Périer, who demanded results, was willing to give Vidocq whatever he wanted, within reason, and the Sûreté promptly expanded: one hundred four persons were on its rolls in Paris, and another fifty-seven served in provincial cities. Their identities were closely guarded, and even Vidocq himself maintained a low profile, making announcements of the capture of criminals in the name of Prefect Gisquet.

The passage of time had not made Vidocq more modest, but he, too, wanted results and was anxious to avoid the limelight. He continued to boast about his exploits when he met authors and other friends for dinner, but it was understood that no information would be leaked to the press and that anything he said had to be regarded as confidential until he retired.

The revitalized Sûreté had its hands full. An epidemic of cholera struck Paris in the spring of 1832, and people of means fled to their country houses while the poor remained behind and perished. On the worst day, April 9, eight hundred fourteen people died. In all, by the time the epidemic ended, more than 17,000 lost their lives.

The uniformed police were as demoralized as the civilian population, and gendarmes of all ranks deserted their posts to join in the exodus from the city. In some districts the personnel was reduced by as much as 60 per cent.

The underworld took full advantage of the chaos. Untenanted homes were emptied of their belongings, pedestrians were no longer safe in even the most fashionable neighborhoods, and pickpockets who mingled with mourners at funerals reaped a golden harvest.

The unemployed added to the panic by throwing up barricades and calling on the people to revolt.

The Sûreté saved Paris, according to a commendation Vidocq received from Louis-Philippe, who gave him a purse of 5000 francs for himself and another of 15,000 francs for his subordinates. The monarch may have exaggerated, but even the bureau's most severe critics had to admit that loyalty and discipline could achieve wonders.

Not one member of the Sûreté left his post of duty during the epidemic. Vidocq worked eighteen hours out of every twenty-four, sleeping on a cot in his office, and his agents followed his example. On its busiest day the bureau was responsible for more than three hundred arrests.

Insurrections broke out in various parts of the city, and both the army and the national guard, their own ranks decimated, responded half-heartedly. The troops sympathized with the rebels, and for a short time it appeared as though Louis-Philippe would be compelled to follow his cousin, Charles X, into exile.

But Vidocq refused to be cowed, bullied or distracted. When a mob gathered to attack the headquarters of the Prefecture, he and eight of his agents, all in disguise, joined in the assault, hauled the ringleaders into the building and placed them under arrest. The crowd melted away. A few days later the members of an artillery battalion dragged cannons into place for the purpose of blasting barricades that had been erected in the Place Vendôme. But the mobs continued to grow, the troops lost heart, and when they began to desert their posts it appeared that the guns would fall into the hands of the rebels. Vidocq was prepared for that emergency, too. He showed up disguised as a colonel of artillery, rallied the troops and forced them to fire a warning shot over the head of the crowd. The insurrectionists lost their appetite for battle and when they took themselves elsewhere Vidocq had the barricades dismantled.

The Chief of the Sûreté submitted a confidential report to Prefect Gisquet, who forwarded it to Minister Périer with a letter of his own, which read:

Among the agents of my administration who displayed the greatest zeal, courage and devotion in suppressing the revolt on the two days of the 5th and 6th of June, I must distinguish the Sieur Vidocq, Head of the Brigade de la Sûreté.

This report, a copy of which I have the honor to address to Your Excellency, will bear witness to the presence of mind and intrepidity shown by this agent at a critical time, and the dangers he ran in defense of public order and the law.

Vidocq ends his report with the request that his sole reward shall be that the King shall know of his conduct.

Your Excellency will decide whether this desire, in itself commendable, can be granted.

Périer sent the report on to the King, and Louis-Philippe responded by making his cash award to Vidocq and his subordinates. It is difficult to suppress the suspicion that the wily Vidocq had calculated the odds and acted accordingly.

The various accounts of Vidocq's life indicate, at least by their omission of amusing stories, that Vidocq was singularly lacking in one quality. But an incident that Gisquet relates in his *Mémoires* proves that the Chief of the Sûreté was indeed endowed with a sense of humor.

One afternoon the Prefect was notified by his secretary that the elderly Duchesse du Châtelet had come to see him on a confidential matter of the greatest importance. The old lady, who lived in a mansion on the faubourg Saint-Germain, was an eccentric and something of a recluse. Few people in positions of authority were acquainted with her, and Gisquet had never met her, but she was reputed to have offered financial encouragement to the republicans, and he was eager to see her.

The Duchess tottered into his office supporting herself with a gold-handled cane, and immediately launched into a long recital of her woes. Her tale was complex and convoluted, and after listening to her for a half-hour the Prefect was thoroughly bewildered.

She noted his confusion and casually mentioned a sensitive, secret assignment that the Prefect had just given Vidocq. Gisquet was startled, wondering how she could have learned of this confidential matter, and inspecting his visitor more closely, discovered that the "Duchesse" was Vidocq, who was enlivening a dull afternoon in his own way.

Gisquet immediately called for his carriage and took the "Duchesse du Châtelet" off to the Tuileries to see King Louis-Philippe. Vidocq maintained his disguise for a half-hour before revealing his real identity and then spent another half-hour with the monarch, who remembered that they had served together in the Bourbon Regiment in the early days of the French Revolution.

Thereafter Vidocq was a frequent visitor to the palace and on these occasions conferred with the King behind closed doors. Presumably he conducted a number of private investigations at Louis-Philippe's request. At no time did he mention these activities to anyone, even after the King lost his throne in 1848. Gisquet was curious, but Vidocq refused to tell him the nature of his private discussions with the crown, and relations between the Prefect and the Chief of the Sûreté became somewhat cooler.

"A detective who is guilty of indiscretion is no detective," Vidocq told Théophile Gautier in later years, and he lived according to his own maxim.

XI

THE PARIS OF THE 1830's was the perfect place for a man who had risen high in the middle class to enjoy life. Louis-Phillipe, a middle-class monarch, as he liked to picture himself, sat on the throne, and men who had earned their own fortunes exercised privileges previously reserved for the aristocrats.

Members of the middle class lived in large homes, and there was a steady construction of new houses in the city and suburbs. The newly wealthy had their own carriages and teams of horses, and cooks, housemaids, butlers and gardeners saw to their comfort. When home cooking palled they could dine in the splendid restaurants that were coming into being all over Paris, establishments that prepared gourmet fare and offered their patrons the finest wines available.

Plays, concerts and operas were presented at twenty-seven theaters, and most performances were sold out. The actors were among the best in the world; the actresses might lack histrionic talents but they were lovely and, like the best wines, were readily available. It was said that every young woman who appeared on the stage had her price.

Sidewalk cafés had existed in Paris for the better part of a century, but they, too, proliferated. Every profession, every trade had its favorites, and this was true of restaurants. It was said that no one other than an author or a physician could win admission to the Grand Vefour, located near the Palais Royal.

Members of the middle class had their clothes made by tailors who had once catered only to aristocrats. Furniture was imported from England, rugs came from the Ottoman Empire and everybody-who-was-anybody decorated his walls with paintings.

A gentlemen, it was said, always carried a walking stick in which a sword was concealed, a silver box that held *cigarros* from Martinique and Guadeloupe, a small vial of cologne to sprinkle on his handkerchief and a pair of white gloves. He dined frequently with friends and associates, attended the theater regularly and never was seen with his wife at late supper, a privilege reserved for his number one mistress of the moment. It was taken for granted, of course, that a gentleman supported at least one mistress.

God was out of fashion, and church attendance languished. Many individual clergyman were popular, however, and those who had private means attended dinner parties and other social functions.

It no longer mattered if one was seen at court or not. Louis-Philippe entertained infrequently, and his parties were regarded as dull because few men of wit and imagination, few women of beauty and charm were invited to the palace.

Money rolled in from every part of the world. New industries were being established in Paris and the smaller cities, new businesses were opening their doors. The sons of the middle class were receiving better education and they moved into the professions as well as into their fathers' offices.

"Paris," observed the American author Washington Irving, just before returning to the United States in 1832 after a long stay in Europe, "offers more pleasure and frivolity to the resident of means and the wealthy visitor than any other city."

Vidocq was a part of the inner circle of Paris but was enjoying few of its fruits. His work required a measure of anonymity that he found increasingly irritating, and his opportunities to join in the gold rush were limited.

On November 15, 1833, he submitted his resignation as Chief of the Brigade de la Sûreté to Prefect Gisquet. His ostensible reason for this sudden act was the illness of his wife, and he mentioned in his letter that he was needed at home to take care of her. He also noted that he was fifty-eight years old and, after the hectic life he had led in recent years, wanted to rest.

He neglected to mention his desire to earn more money.

What he also failed to say in his letter was that he had been under pressure from Minister Périer and Prefect Gisquet to reform the Brigade de la Sûreté. Many people, including a number of magistrates and prominent attorneys, felt the time had come for the bureau to get rid of the former convicts on its payroll. Their motives were simple: Vidocq himself could control the ex-prisoners, but experience had shown that many of them had gained by graft and otherwise taken advantage of their position during the years of his previous retirement. Some day he would leave, and far-sighted critics didn't want the organization to fall apart again.

Vidocq flatly refused to accept the arguments of the reformers. He had demonstrated that the Brigade de la Sûreté could perform vital functions when it employed former criminals, he said, and in his opinion only a thief knew the tricks of the trade sufficiently well to catch a thief. When Gisquet pointed out that a number of agents who were successful had been recruited from the ranks of the uniformed police, Vidocq replied that they were responsible for fewer arrests than were the ex-convicts on his staff.

A few years later Vidocq explained his position in a private, indignant letter to Victor Hugo. "It was my belief that to keep the criminals down one had to use men who knew them and had lived among them," he wrote. "Deprived of such tools I felt reduced to impotence. I refused to sacrifice them, so I resigned and left the police."

Every effort was made on both sides to present the appearance of an amicable parting. Vidocq was given a pension equal to his salary at retirement, and this fact was publicized. Few people ever found out that the payments were erratic and that they stopped completely after a few years.

One of the last services Vidocq performed before his retirement was the recommendation of a competent man to succeed him. Pierre Allard, who had started his career as a gendarme, had spent a number of years as a Sûreté agent before returning to the uniformed police, where he had risen to the rank of commissaire. A new position, that of chief inspector, was also created and was given to another Vidocq protégé, Louis Canler.

But these men were hampered, at least initially, by a new regulation that forbade the Sûreté to employ any man who had a criminal record. Thanks to Vidocq's last-minute intervention before his departure, however, the bureau retained the right to pay for information it received from undercover sources, including criminals. In spite of this safeguard the Brigade de la Sûreté suffered and, for at least five years, its achievements were minimal. Thereafter, as new agents became more proficient, its record gradually improved.

Vidocq was never satisfied with its accomplishments. For the next twelve years he dined with Allard regularly and gave him advice, but never failed to emphasize that a Sûreté without former convicts on its payroll was a crippled bureau. Sometimes he was persecuted by Allard, too, but always knew his former aide was just following orders.

The problem that faced Vidocq after he left the police a second time was how to occupy himself. He could have retired at fifty-eight, an age regarded as elderly by his contemporaries. His home in Saint-Mandé was comfortable, he had recouped the small fortune he had lost when his paper-box factory had failed, and his moneylending business still earned him a substantial income. If necessary he could have sold his taverns in the slum district, too, for a large profit.

The thought of actual retirement did not cross Vidocq's mind. He enjoyed robust health, his energies and appetites were undiminished and his mind was alert. For years he had enjoyed both power and fame and he had no intention of abandoning either for the bucolic pleasures of his little country estate.

As the world soon would learn, Vidocq had already made careful plans for his future. Louis-Philippe was still being called the "bourgeouis King," and France was more prosperous than ever before. Middle-class merchants, bankers, traders and manufacturers were becoming millionaires, and even little shopkeepers were enjoying unprecedented wealth. As a consequence the country was flooded with swindlers, forgers, confidence men and other criminals who schemed to separate them from their money.

Vidocq, the man who knew more about their techniques and more about them as individuals than anyone in history, the man who utilized scientific techniques to catch and convict criminals, established the world's first private detective agency on January 3, 1834.

The Anglo-Saxon world has given that honor to Alan Pinkerton, a Scotsman who emigrated to the United States in 1842, became deputy sheriff of Cook County, Illinois, and in 1850 opened his own detective agency in Chicago. The Anglo-Saxon dates were wrong because Vidocq preceded Pinkerton by sixteen and one-half years.

Calling his new operation Le Bureau des Renseignements, or the Information Bureau, Vidocq opened a suite of offices at 12, rue Cloche-Perce, off the rue de Rivoli. He employed fourteen persons, including two clerks, a private secretary and eleven detectives. Most of his agents were themselves former criminals, and a number of them had served prison terms as swindlers.

Advertising extensively in the press and through single-sheet fliers that well-dressed young men handed out at the entrances to banks and other financial institutions, Vidocq made it clear from the outset that he intended to specialize in credit services. His clients would enjoy the benefits to be obtained from the information in his files, which contained data on many thousands of swindlers and other criminals.

He promised that all investigations would be confidential and said that when a client wanted credit information on an individual it would be supplied promptly. Five thousand swindlers were preying on the innocent in Paris, and thousands of others were at work in the provinces, fleecing honest citizens of their hard-earned money. Vidocq's customers would know before they did business with a man whether he was honest or not.

The fees charged by the Information Bureau were surprisingly modest. Individuals paid five francs for a single meeting, twenty-five for a retainer fee of one year, during which time they could call as often as they wished. Companies, depending on their size, paid anywhere from twenty francs to fifty for a single meeting and from one hundred to one thousand francs for a year's retainer fee.

Even before opening his doors Vidocq made certain his new venture would succeed. Among his first clients who signed contracts with him in advance were three banks, an investment house that sold bonds, a shipping line and two large hotels, one in Paris and the other in Lyons. Other clients, attracted by his reputation, soon flocked to him, and he had to expand before he had been in business more than three months.

The assistant director of the Information Bureau was a former commissaire of the Paris police, Alfred Lucas, who wrote novels in his spare time. It is probable that he was the actual author of various articles and other works that began to appear in print under Vidocq's name. Another employee with a literary bent was Leo Lespès, who later wrote lightly humorous articles for several Paris newspapers. He was hired as

Vidocq's secretary and served in that capacity for several years. It is safe to assume that he, too, was the author of various pieces published under Vidocq's name.

The police were outraged when the inauguration of the Information Bureau was announced but quickly discovered that they were powerless to close its doors. Vidocq had taken the precaution of hiring attorneys who had made an exhaustive check at the Ministry of Justice, and there was no law that prevented the operation. The uniformed police fumed, and only Allard, the new head of the Brigade de la Sûreté, was pleased, saying it was a relief that Vidocq intended to do his work for him.

Functioning as he had when he had worked for the government, Vidocq sent agents into the underworld in disguise, sometimes making such forays himself, and paid criminals for authentic information. He still followed the policy of keeping his sources strictly confidential, and he always kept his word because he knew the value of such tactics. His informants used a rear entrance and were never seen by clients.

In addition to supplying credit information on individuals, the new organization also functioned as a debt collecting agency, Vidocq thereby expanding a service he had provided for many years to a few customers. Now anyone willing to pay a fee could come to him for that purpose.

It was inevitable, perhaps, that the Information Bureau should branch out into other fields. The proprietor of a large shop discovered that money was missing from the till regularly but had no way of knowing which of his employees was robbing him. One of Vidocq's assistants joined the staff as a clerk, and the thief was apprehended in a few days. Quantities of metal were vanishing from the warehouse of a company that made pots and pans, so one of the agency's operatives went to work there disguised as a laborer and soon caught two senior employees who were taking the metal, then reselling it to the proprietor through a third party.

Unsolicited clients began to come to Vidocq for help in solving domestic problems, from that day to the present a detective agency staple. A husband or wife suspected his or her spouse of infidelity and hired the Information Bureau to obtain the facts. A husband disappeared from home, and his wife, uncertain whether he was running away or had met with foul play, paid Vidocq to trace him. A suitor vanished with a young heiress, and her parents brought in the Information Bureau to locate the couple and bring their daughter home.

Most of these cases were routine, easy to solve and paid well. After a year Vidocq estimated that they took care of his payroll and basic office expenses. They offered him no challenge because most could be handled by his assistants without his personal intervention, freeing him for more complex cases.

It was at about this time that Vidocq began to collect paintings. His original intention was the decoration of his offices, and his personal tastes were macabre. Balzac, after paying his first visit to the office, wrote a short, descriptive essay about it for a newspaper. He had been horrified, he said, by a huge painting behind Vidocq's desk that depicted the beheading of John the Baptist. Turning away from it, he was shocked again when he saw, on the opposite wall, a painting of Joan of Arc being burned at the stake. One of Vidocq's own favorites, which disgusted many of his visitors, was a depiction in oils of a mangled corpse.

Most of the gruesome pictures were confined to Vidocq's own anterooms and private office. More conventional paintings lined the other walls, and portraits of various Ministers of the Police and Interior, Prefects of Paris police and other officials were on display in the reception room.

Vidocq already had a valuable collection of silver, and it may have been Balzac, himself a lover of material possessions, who persuaded him to invest in paintings on a large scale. Regardless of whether he provided the original spark or not, Balzac maintained a lively interest in Vidocq's new enthusiasm.

Knowing nothing about art, Vidocq nevertheless knew what he liked and made his purchases accordingly. In addition to the gruesome he liked nudes, portraits of beautiful women and of strong, virile men. He owned no paintings by any artist of renown, apparently preferring unknowns whose works he could buy inexpensively.

Over the years he filled the house in Saint-Mandé with paintings, then covered the walls of the various apartments he rented in Paris, too. Although lacking in discrimination he was proud of his paintings, always showing them to visitors and taking umbrage when they were not admired.

By the time of his death his collection had more than doubled in value, not because any of the paintings were recognized as masterpieces, but simply because he owned so many. In 1856, the year before he died, he had more than 2000. By that time all but a few had been packed in boxes and were gathering dust in a friend's attic.

In spite of their lack of merit the paintings help illuminate Vidocq's character. He enjoyed and appreciated them, just as he liked the company of writers. He was neither adopting a pose nor seeking publicity when he bought paintings, and Balzac said he showed them only to friends, not to customers.

Publicity was still his lifeblood, however, and was largely responsible for the continuing success and expansion of his detective agency. Reporters could always come to him for a colorful, exciting story that made good reading, even though he paid scant attention to fact and exaggerated wildly when telling about a recent case.

In December, 1836, he had a second flier printed, and in it he claimed that the Information Bureau was responsible for cutting the illegal profits of French swindlers by one-third. He cited no authority for these startling statistics, but he did list the names of more than forty satisfied clients, among them banks, attorneys, bond sellers and manufacturers. All, he stressed, currently were represented by the agency on retainer fees.

The extraordinary growth of the Information Bureau inspired others to imitate him, and by 1836 there were a number of other detective agencies in Paris. Chief among them were The Tocsin, The Illuminator and The Lighthouse, and late in that year almost a score of others opened and then closed their doors. Vidocq's competitors were either incompetents or criminals and failed or were closed by the authorities. The partners in The Lighthouse were sentenced to a year in prison for fraud, while the owners of The Illuminator and The Tocsin were convicted of blackmail.

In his flier Vidocq happily revealed the details of his venture:

> My daily exponses are 100 francs, which accumulates to a total of 36,500 francs per year. Yet, although I only charge my subscribers and clients a modest fee, based on the importance of the business they bring me, my business yields 15,000 to 20,000 francs per year clear profit.

He went on to explain that when it was necessary for an investigation to be made, the client paid its expenses as well as an extra fee. He offered his customers special plaques to nail to their doors, saying they were under the protection of "Vidocq's Information Bureau." The small sum they would be charged for a plaque was a minor expense because, he explained, no criminal in France would dare to rob or burglarize a place that he and his competent assistants were guarding.

He also revealed in the flier, casually, that he now had more than 3000 regular clients who paid him annual fees.

Neither this figure nor any of the other statistics appear to have been exaggerated. In 1859, two years after Vidocq's death, Théophile Gautier declared in the column he wrote regularly for *Le Moniteur universel* that he had access to the great detective's financial ledgers for the period and that the claims were accurate. No other individual, he said, had ever enjoyed the complete confidence of so many of his fellow citizens, and no other man had so richly deserved their trust.

In 1836 Vidocq forcefully called himself to the attention of the public by appearing as the author of a new book, *Les Voleurs*, or, *The Thieves*, which he published himself. This work, a compilation of the alleged case histories of various super-robbers, burglars, swindlers and confidence men he had placed behind bars, bore little relation to real life. The criminals were super-fiends, but Vidocq — the mastermind who was the prototype for Sherlock Holmes, Inspector Maigret and scores of other magnified detective heroes in European and Anglo-Saxon literature — was even more clever, intrepid and ingenious than his arch foes, and always triumphed.

Most of the tales told in *The Thieves* stretched credulity to the breaking point, characterizations were absurd, and the book's style was lurid and verbose, bearing little or no relation to the style of his *Mémoires*. Alfred Lucas happened to be in Vidocq's employ at this time, and the convoluted, sometimes tortured style bore a strong similarity to that of Lucas's own novels, two of which were advertised in the final pages of *The Thieves*.

The actual authorship of the latest work to be attributed to Vidocq, *The Thieves*, is of little importance. It was written and published to make money and to publicize the Information Bureau and it achieved both goals admirably. More than 35,000 copies were sold in the first year, and another 20,000 were purchased in 1838. Regardless of whether Vidocq, Lucas or a third person actually wrote the book, the founder of the Brigade de la Sûreté established yet another record by becoming the world's first author of best-selling detective fiction.

The format of *The Thieves* has been utilized in countless whodunits. Each story — or supposed case history — was a mystery in which the reader was deliberately challenged, and was invited not only to match wits with the criminal but with the great Vidocq who solved the case by outsmarting the villain. Aristocrats and physicians, lawyers and business-men played the game with gusto.

Published in two volumes for the very high price of fifteen francs, the book had a full title that gave its flavor: *The Thieves, Physiology of Their Lives and Language. A Work Which Unveils the Ruses of All the Rogues, Destined to Be-come the Living Dictionary of All Honest Men.*

Vidocq was necessarily the guiding force in the book's preparation because it was filled with literally thousands of details that only a great criminologist could have known. He explained with almost frightening accuracy the tricks used by swindlers, confidence men and card sharks. He told how thieves could break into supposedly burglarproof homes, of-fices and factories by using short swords, fashioned in Spain of the finest Toledo steel and then honed to razor sharpness, which would facilitate the slicing of even the strongest metal bars. He outlined the methods used by pickpockets who filed their fingertips in order to acquire a sensitivity of touch de-nied to ordinary citizens.

He warned the patrons of brothels that they were often kept under watch through secret peepholes and that the con-tents of their wallets were removed by silent accomplices while they were being entertained — and distracted — by the inmates.

He told the unwary that robbers carried knives with thin handles and very thin blades beneath their sleeves, loosely bound to their arms, and he explained how these weapons, the precursors of the twentieth-century switchblade, could be dropped into a man's waiting hand by a mere shake of the arm. Women were robbers, too, and hid their knives in the soles of their shoes, special compartments having been built into their footgear for this purpose.

Forgers often opened a seemingly innocent correspondence with intended victims in order to obtain samples of their signatures. Card cheats marked decks of playing cards with tiny dots on the backs, almost invisible and meaningless to anyone else.

One of the favorite tricks of a burglar was that of obtaining employment in a home, then actually working there for a week or two, and during that time learning the hiding places of money, jewels and other valuables. Frequently burglars used accomplices who remained in the employ of the victims.

He listed the superstitions of criminals of all classes and, naming names, he drew vivid word pictures of taverns, restaurants, inns and hotels in Paris and the provinces that catered to the underworld. As Balzac remarked, any police officer who failed to read the book and memorize the information it contained was a fool.

Vidocq forcefully presented his favorite theme, later enlarged by Eugène Sue and adopted by liberals in many countries, that the criminal was not congenitally bad. Poverty and emotional deprivations had confused the criminal, Vidocq declared, and insisted that by treating him as a human being and trusting him he could be rehabilitated.

In *The Thieves* Vidocq also launched a sharp attack on what he regarded as a national scandal, the treatment accorded vagabonds by the government. A vagabond, he said, was no more and no less than a man who had lost his employment and, without funds, was forced to wander from place to place. Under the law he could be arrested and imprisoned by gendarmes for as long as three months and then could be sentenced to a prison term for an additional six months. The innocent vagabond associated with hardened criminals in the jails and, by the time he emerged, he, too, had become a criminal. Vidocq insisted that the system had to be changed.

In the preface to *The Thieves* Vidocq discussed himself and the legends about him with engaging candor:

By the nature of my occupation from 1809 to 1827, and because of my previous relationships, there was an obstinate and incessant fight between me and those I was charged to pursue. Many men therefore had a direct interest in damaging me, and as my enemies were not the kind to use white gloves, they said to each other, "Let us slander and slander again; some of it will always stick."

At this moment, if I am to believe those who do not know me, I am a freak, an anamoly, a fairy tale giant — everything and anything imaginable, no matter how vile, disgusting or contrary to the very elements of human nature it might be.

My friends have reacted to these distortions with magnifications of their own. They make me out to be a knight in armor, the hero of a new Crusade, a modern Saint George who slays the dragons of the nether regions. This, too, is sheer rubbish.

They say I have the gift of tonguos and the ring of Gyges; like another Proteus I can assume whatever form pleaoor me; I am the hero of a thousand ridiculous tales. What nonsense! Let me assure you, reader, that I — like you — am mortal. If my veins are cut I will bleed, if my throat is slashed, I will die . . .

Several times during my career, prejudice has barred my path, but it is above all since I founded the business I direct today that I have been best able to appreciate its sinister power. How many people have lost more or less considerable sums because they did not come and ask my advice? Because, written on my office door is: VIDOCQ!

Even more important to Vidocq's reputation and the maintenance of his image was his appearance in the books of his friends. The first to use his character, background and experiences was Balzac. Thinly disguised at Inspector Vautrin in *Le Père Goriot*, which was serialized in 1834 and published the next year, Vidocq proved so popular that Balzac used him again in novel after novel.

Vidocq's influence on Victor Hugo was also profound, but it was his ideas regarding justice and the need for prison reforms that influenced the great novelist and poet. *Les Mi-*

sérables, on which Hugo worked intermittently for a number of years, was not published until 1862, five years after Vidocq's death, but the author's debt to his old friend is clear.

These same principles, repeatedly espoused by Vidocq at his dinners with friends, helped inspire Eugène Sue. Two of his most successful works, *Les Mystères de Paris,* published in 1843, and *Le Juif errant,* which appeared two years later, were long, rambling and enormously exciting works of fiction that presented Vidocq's ideas with greater force and clarity than he himself had done. It should be noted, too, that the *Mystères de Paris* influenced Hugo when he was writing *Les Misérables.*

Alexandre Dumas the elder borrowed from Vidocq in his own blithe way, as he borrowed from everyone. He said that his great romantic novel, *Le Comte de Monte-Cristo,* was inspired by Vidocq, but the connection was clear to no one except Dumas himself. Perhaps something that Vidocq said at dinner one evening sparked him; in any event, Vidocq was inundated with congratulations when *Monte-Cristo* was published in 1844.

Dumas's debt to him is direct and unmistakable in the detective novels he wrote from 1839 to 1841. These stories, first published separately and then under the collective title *Crimes célèbres,* borrowed openly from previous books by and about Vidocq. Cases on which he had worked were used and enlarged, and the famous detective appeared in them, with only his name changed. His personality and appearance, his idiosyncrasies and habits were taken without apology from real life.

In the period from 1853 to 1857 Dumas again leaned on Vidocq after suffering financial vicissitudes caused by his prodigal expenditures. Returning from France after going into self-imposed exile to escape from his creditors, Dumas founded a daily newspaper, *Le Mousquetaire,* which specialized in literary and dramatic criticism. As was his custom he wrote most of the articles himself, under a variety of pseudonyms, but had trouble filling the newspaper's columns. So he wrote another long series of pieces about the exploits of a master detective who happened to bear a striking resemblance to Vidocq.

Vidocq had the good sense not to protest when his distinguished friends used him, his career and his ideas in their books. These works added to his fame and delighted him, in spite of his assumed modesty in the preface to *The Thieves*. By the late 1830's, when Vidocq was in his sixties, he was riding the crest of a wave of renown.

XII

ON JULY 24, 1838, Vidocq celebrated his sixty-third birthday by moving his offices to new quarters at 20, rue du Pont Louis-Philippe, but his business continued to expand so rapidly that before the year ended he was compelled to move yet again, establishing the Information Bureau in a large building of its own at 39, rue Neuve-Saint-Eustache. "Eight omnibus routes pass our door!" the office stationery boasted.

By any standards the success of the detective agency was phenomenal, and there were now sixty persons on the payroll, serving in four separate divisions. The precise duties of each were known only to staff members, Vidocq being reluctant to allow swindlers and other criminals to learn his organizational secrets. Certainly his clients didn't care; all that mattered to them was that he produced results.

One division is known to have investigated robberies and burglaries, although that fact was not advertised. The Sûreté, under Allard, was doing all it could to fight crime, but the absence of ex-convicts on its staff had taken a toll, and it was far less efficient than it had been. The uniformed police were still sloppy, negligent and unable to cope with any but the most elementary crimes.

People who wanted to recover money or property that had been stolen went in vain to the authorities, then began to turn to Vidocq for help. He was happy to oblige them, charging only a percentage of the sums he recovered. If the Information Bureau failed in such a mission, he and his staff received nothing for their work. This arrangement was so eminently fair that people of modest means as well as the wealthy came to the Information Bureau for help.

Vidocq's men, many of them Brigade de la Sûreté graduates, used the same techniques they had employed when they had worked for the government, and case after case was solved. No statistics are available because Vidocq kept them secret, but thousands of Parisians knew that if their money or valuables were stolen, the Information Bureau would recover their property. The division became the biggest and most profitable in the Information Bureau.

The very existence of the division galled the police. Both the Sûreté and the uniformed branches were mortified when Vidocq's "rogues" brought in a robber or burglar for whom the gendarmes had been searching. They spoke disparagingly of Vidocq's private police force and tried to muster public opinion against the Information Bureau, but the people shrugged off their efforts. "When the police arrest as many people as M. Vidocq," Hugo said in an essay published in *La Presse* in November, 1838, "perhaps he will be persuaded to retire. But until that day comes, long may he remain active! Paris needs him, France needs him, and we recommend that the gendarmes drink their sour wine."

The workrooms in the new offices, which included a laboratory equipped with chemicals and magnifying glasses, were bare, uncluttered and resembled the old Sûreté headquarters. These portions of the building, as well as the elaborate files stored in the cellar, were never visited by clients, and even employees were not encouraged to wander beyond the perimeters of their respective divisions.

The public rooms were magnificent, and Vidocq had enlisted the aid of his wife in their decoration. The furniture had been made to order in Paris, the wallpaper and drapes had come from a factory in Lyons, several tapestries had been purchased in Brussels and the thick rugs came from the

Ottoman Empire. Balzac approved of the splendor, and Dumas, making his first tour, announced that he was jealous.

An exceptionally pretty young woman was on duty in the reception room, and it was taken for granted that she was Vidocq's current mistress, but for once the gossips were mistaken. Her name was Marie Dupont, and she happened to be Mme. Vidocq's niece on her father's side. After working at the Information Bureau for several years Mlle. Dupont married a senior agent.

Visitors of consequence were conducted to the offices of the Director and his principal assistants by a liveried page, and clients were quick to observe that the floors in the corridors were carpeted and that the walls were paneled.

It was rumored that Vidocq used a desk that had belonged to Napoleon, but he was too sensible to encourage the Bonapartists when a Bourbon sat on the throne. His office was dominated by his hideous painting of the beheading of John the Baptist, and Balzac, who thought it revolting, laughed when he heard that Vidocq had rejected a price of 75,000 francs for it. He said that he himself wouldn't pay seven sous for it other than for the pleasure of destroying it.

During Vidocq's second tour of duty at the Sûreté he had formed the habit of dictating memoranda and letters in order to save time, and he continued this practice at the Information Bureau. His secretaries necessarily developed their own crude systems of shorthand, as he spoke rapidly. No real method of abbreviating had yet been devised, but the secretaries took great care not to make mistakes. Vidocq was a stickler for accuracy, and although he had the faculty of remaining calm in difficult situations, he could lose his temper with subordinates when they erred.

He became so enamored of dictation as a device that, soon after the establishment of the Information Bureau, he introduced a new and — at the time — revolutionary practice: major clients visiting the office for the first time were urged to explain their problems in their own words, with Vidocq or a senior assistant interjecting questions when required for the sake of clarification.

A secretary took down a verbatim account of the case, precisely as the client described it. Later the customer was shown a transcribed copy and had the right to make any corrections he wished. This innovation, Vidocq believed, made it possible for him and his agents to make their investigations with greater ease and facility, and they could keep the client's desires in mind at all times.

Senior agents working on complex cases also had the privilege of dictating notes, memoranda and progress reports to special clerks who had been hired to perform that function. Files were kept up to date, and if an agent had to be taken off a case for any reason, his replacement could step in without difficulty.

Gautier, who thought Vidocq could do no wrong, indicated in a newspaper article written in 1858 that the master detective had been the first to use dictation regularly as a matter of policy. But the author-critic claimed too much for his friend. Busy men had been dictating letters and memoranda to aides for centuries. The most that can be said for Vidocq is that he may have been one of the first businessmen of his era to utilize dictation on a large scale as a means of increasing efficiency.

The Information Bureau ledgers for May and June, 1838, which are still extant and repose in the archives of the Bibliothèque Nationale, tell a great deal about Vidocq's operations. As has already been seen, he employed a large staff by this time, but he kept his financial accounts himself, writing them in his own hand. Apparently he wanted no subordinate to know too much about the agency's income.

One client, the owner of a large shop, paid the whopping sum of 2000 francs in May and another 1200 francs in June for the expenses incurred by agents conducting surveillances. There is no explanation given, but in June the proprietor also paid the agency a fee of 2500 francs. Obviously the case was important.

There are glimpses, too, of an unpublicized aspect of Vidocq's complex personality in his ledger. One customer, identified only as Mme. Louise Alford, came to him in the hope that he could collect the sum of twenty-five francs owed to her by a restaurant for services rendered as a cook. Vidocq accepted the case, collected the money and then refused to charge Mme. Alford either a commission or a fee, instead giving her the entire amount. Twenty-five francs wasn't very much money but must have been important to the cook, and the detective refused to take a few francs from her.

When he regarded it as necessary he did not hesitate to go to court on behalf of clients and sue for debts. Consequently he appeared frequently before the magistrates, and his cases were so thoroughly documented that he almost always won them. When he had difficulty in collecting from his own clients he went to court for that money, too, and his enemies never proved their claim that he sometimes used strong-arm methods.

Occasionally he encountered problems caused by his own employees. One incident, which the police used in a vain attempt to discredit him, involved an agent named Maurice who was assigned to keep watch on a shop owned by a man called Sauvelet. Apparently Maurice was less than expert at the art of surveillance because Sauvelet realized what he was doing and challenged him.

Maurice replied that he was being paid three francs per day for the job, but he offered to desist and reveal the name of his employer in return for a fee of one hundred francs. Sauvelet said the price was too high.

The next day Maurice returned and reduced his demand to forty francs. Two gendarmes who were hidden on the premises arrested him, and when they reached the police station

Maurice announced that he was a member of the Information Bureau staff.

Maurice was tried, and Vidocq appeared in court to testify. He swore that the agent had acted on his own authority, and as the prosecution could not prove to the contrary, Vidocq won exoneration. But the results of the case did not satisfy him. He told friends he suspected that Maurice actually had been a double agent, working for the police, who had set a trap for their enemy.

This charge could be dismissed as an example of a persecution complex since Vidocq frequently spoke of his foes, were it not for later developments. In November, 1839, the Sûreté and the uniformed police arrested four employees of the Ministry of War who were charged with stealing official documents. The newspapers hinted that Vidocq was involved, quoting anonymous sources to the effect that the Information Bureau maintained close liaison with many government departments, and that Vidocq frequently borrowed official papers. The security of the state allegedly was involved.

Libel laws were virtually non-existent, and the press enjoyed itself thoroughly for the sake of increased circulation at the expense of Vidocq's good name. Several of the smaller, less responsible newspapers hinted broadly that the master detective was actually a master spy in the employ of a foreign power. Anonymous sources were cited to the effect that the success of the Information Bureau was due to huge fees Vidocq supposedly received from the unnamed foreign nation.

Vidocq's friends rallied to him, but he shrugged aside their concern. As yet he had no idea that the police intended to make a serious effort to discredit him and close his doors permanently.

It was said that a number of government departments were under investigation, but the Prefecture refused to confirm or deny the rumors. No one in a position of authority would comment, either, on the allegation that a number of additional civil servants were also under arrest.

Four days after the initial move the Sûreté made a sudden, surprise raid on the Information Bureau, carrying off more than 3500 individual files. The newspapers gleefully reported that more than half were secret Sûreté documents that, in some mysterious manner, had found their way into private hands.

Morning newspapers announced on November 30 that Vidocq had been taken into custody. He was seen in the corridors and main lobby of the Ministry of Justice that same morning, however, so afternoon newspapers announced that the rumor was untrue.

On the evening of November 30 Vidocq granted the press an interview and announced that he was innocent. No documents that were government property had been found in his files for the simple reason that none had ever been stored there or anywhere else.

The police made a grave mistake. Under the law the seized papers should have been sealed in the presence of the Procurator General, the principal government prosecutor, to prevent tampering, and should have been given intact to the Chief Examining Magistrate for safekeeping. In his interview Vidocq brought the error to the attention of the public.

The following day the police tried to cover up for themselves by sending Vidocq an order to appear at the Prefecture for the purpose of witnessing the examination of the seized documents.

Vidocq refused, and on December 2 wrote a blistering letter of complaint to the Procurator General. The police had taken liberties that the Chief Examining Magistrate himself would not have taken. His papers, unprotected and subject to tampering and other mischief, had been in the hands of the police for one week, and the Prefecture was assuming authority that belonged exclusively to the courts. He concluded in anger:

I need not tell you, M. le Procurator General, that I am not novice enough, an old veteran like me, to condone such irregularities by my presence. Vidocq was not born to fall into these gentlemen's snares. It would be far too amusing. He will therefore permit the gentlemen to take their time classifying, falsifying and otherwise changing the dossiers that have already been in their possession for so many days.

Copies of this communication were sent to the newspapers, which printed them, and Vidocq took full advantage of the edge he had won in what was developing into a public-relations battle. The following day he sent a longer, formal communication to the Procurator General. Dumas may have had a hand in revising and editing this document; in any event, he was present when Vidocq called in the press and read it aloud. He said, in part:

Is it because my name is Vidocq that the police think themselves authorized to be unjust? Is it because my name is Vidocq that I come to ask the courts for prompt and public justice? What has drawn the hatred of the police upon me? I ask you to ponder this question, M. le Procurator General, and I ask my fellow citizens to ponder with you.

Might it be my former, always loyal services? Have they forgotten that for twenty years, at the constant risk of my life, I brought to justice the most dangerous robbers and assassins?

Whatever the pretext for the outrageous vexation inflicted upon me, it is unjust and disloyal.

You already know, M. le Procurator General, of my refusal to attend the farcical proceedings at the Prefecture. I have the honor, now, to inform you further that I have now entered legal proceedings against the four commissaires directly responsible for the violation of my rights.

Be further informed that I have now had an opportunity to study my files and therefore have ascertained at least some portion of the materials illegally taken from me. A portion of the confiscated documents consists of notes and drafts of reports furnished by me to the various Prefects of police, at their request, while I was performing the duties of Chief of the Brigade de la

Sûreté. In many instances these notes directly relate to people who are still in the service of the police, and who, therefore, are now in a position to be the judges of their own cause.

Sir, in the name of the King's justice I beg you to remove this entire matter from the hands of the prejudiced police and to deal with it yourself!

Any officials who had thought Vidocq would accept the seizure meekly and without doing battle to the fullest extent of his considerable ability didn't know their opponent. He visited the Ministry of Justice daily to confer with many officials with whom he had been friendly for years. On December 18 he filed a second suit against the commissaires, in which he made the flat charge that by now they could have "altered or otherwise deformed" his dossiers in any way they pleased.

On December 19 he took the daring step of filing yet another suit, this one against the Prefect of police himself. A new man had just been appointed to the office and was an unknown quantity: Paul Delessert was a businessman who had not been associated with the police previously, and there is nothing in the records to indicate that he and Vidocq had been acquainted. The seizure could not have been made without the knowledge and approval of the new Prefect, of course, so Vidocq was waging personal war on him, too. The move took courage.

That was just the beginning. Paris was astonished when Vidocq went on to hire Charles Ledru, the man almost universally regarded as the best lawyer in Paris, to defend his interests. Charles Ledru was also a controversial figure, simultaneously a devout Roman Catholic and an outspoken advocate of republicanism. He dressed in the latest fashions, was a deadly swordsman and reputedly was a ladies' man. He despised Vidocq, supposedly because an attractive actress in whom he had been interested preferred the attentions of the detective.

A copy of Ledru's reply to Vidocq's request for representation appeared in his own *Mémoires:*

I would not refuse my services to anyone to whom they could be of use. I must inform you in candor, however, that you do not inspire in me sufficient interest for me to defend you without charging a fee.

On the other hand, you will understand that no French advocate can accept a fee from Vidocq.

I see no way of reconciling your request with my scruples unless it should be agreeable to you to take the Sisters of Saint Vincent de Paul the sum of 1000 francs, which I fix as the figure which would normally be due to me in the event I accepted your case.

Vidocq's reply, which also appears in Ledru's *Mémoires,* was prompt:

I chose you to defend me because you are one of the advocates who attacked my actions, when I held public office, most firmly and consistently.

I recall that fact not only to ask for your support in my present situation. I want my counsel to be my first judge, and my most severe. I need only tell you that I have nothing to fear.

I accept, sir, the condition that you impose . . .

I shall have the honor of calling on you, if you will allow me, between three and five o'clock this afternoon. Your secretary informs me that you can be seen at that time.

Promptly at 3:00 P.M. Vidocq called on Ledru, placing on the lawyer's desk a receipt signed by one Sister Henriette of the Sisters of Saint Vincent de Paul. The document stated that M. Vidocq had made a gift to the convent of 2500 francs.

That was the beginning of a close relationship with Ledru that would last until the end of their lives. Now they were prepared to do battle together, and the alliance was formed just in time.

On December 23, when Vidocq returned to his office from an errand, he was informed that three gentlemen awaited him. They were Chief of the Sûreté, Allard, Chief Inspector of the Sûreté, Canler and a commissaire named Jennison. They presented him with an order for his arrest signed by one of the few members of the bench with whom he was not well acquainted, Examining Magistrate Fleury.

Vidocq was unperturbed. "Well, gentlemen," he was later quoted by Victor Hugo as saying, "at last you are satisfied. Allow me to inform you that my satisfaction is even greater." Obviously he believed the authorities had gone too far in their campaign against him.

He was escorted to the small Sainte-Pélagie Prison in Paris, where he was confined in a private cell, with guards stationed outside the door to prevent attacks on him by criminals who were also lodged there. On Christmas Day Mme. Vidocq brought him a roast goose and other delicacies in a basket, and was permitted to dine with him.

Vidocq had no way, under the law, of winning his release prior to his trial; under the legal system of the period no man was freed on bail. So he spent the entire holiday season in jail.

XIII

THE POLICE were thorough, and their charges against Vidocq, which were published on December 29, 1839, plainly indicated their intention of closing the doors of the Information Bureau for all time. The bill of particulars against the defendant listed three counts, all of them far more serious than the original charge that government documents had been found in his possession. The first was that he obtained money from clients under false pretenses: in other words, he was a swindler. The second accused him of deliberately corrupting government employees. The third accused him, as Director of the Information Agency, of "usurping public functions." The bill did not name the law that this alleged usurpation broke.

On January 4, 1840, Vidocq, with the help of Advocate Ledru, wrote a long letter to the judge who had been assigned the case, Examining Magistrate P.-P. Legonidec, one of the younger members of the bench with whom — through no coincidence — he was not acquainted. In it he outlined his career, saying he had been responsible for the arrest and conviction of 20,000 criminals. His achievements had aroused the jealousy of the police, he stressed, and they hated him more than did the men he had sent to prison.

This communication was the cause of a sharp dispute between Vidocq and his lawyer, the former insisting that copies be released to the press, the latter refusing because he was afraid the judge might be offended. Ledru could be as stubborn as Vidocq, and they argued bitterly, but the lawyer won because his client had no direct access to reporters.

Vidocq apologized effusively in a letter that appeared in Ledru's *Mémoires:*

> Diogenes, philosopher of Cynic memory, lantern in hand, sought an honest man throughout Athens and found him not.
>
> Happier than he, I have found one in the modern Babylon whom I love and respect. That man is you, Charles Ledru.
>
> Please, sir, do not forget that the respect of Vidocq is a cross of merit which very few people possess.

The trial began on January 16 and lasted until February 27. Magistrate Legonidec was conscientious, and, because of the public interest in the case, he was thorough. A total of three hundred fifty-two witnesses testified, about two-thirds of them called by the defense.

One of the most prominent witnesses was Chief Examining Magistrate Henri Zangiacomi, who made it clear that in his opinion Vidocq was a great man. Three other magistrates testified in the same vein, as did the Procurator General, Claude Franck-Carré, who indicated that both as the government prosecutor and privately as an attorney he believed the police lacked sufficient evidence to prove their charges. He also spoke at length from the witness stand about the valuable services Vidocq had performed for the state.

The outcome of the trial was never in doubt, the two young prosecutors assigned to the case openly admitting that the evidence accumulated by the police was circumstantial and vague. On February 27th Vidocq was not only acquitted after spending two months in prison, but the court praised him as a man of honor and stature.

Vidocq's celebration had already been prepared in the form of thousands of posters, previously printed, with a huge banner headline at the top that proclaimed: **LIBERTY!** This poster, distributed throughout Paris by the thousands, told current customers and potential clients that the Director of the Information Bureau was taking personal charge of his agency again, and to prevent impostors from harming the public, his agents, henceforth, would carry special credentials bearing his signature.

In this same oversized poster Vidocq also announced the removal of his offices to a new address, 13, Galerie Vivienne. The Galerie was an arcade lined on both sides with some of the city's most exclusive, expensive shops frequented principally by newly rich members of the middle class. On one side of the Information Bureau was a bookstore, and on the other a shop that sold perfume and cosmetics. Directly across the arcade were a dressmaking establishment and a bootmaker.

A doorman who carried a sword and a concealed pistol was on duty at the Information Bureau entrance at all times, and visitors climbed a flight of iron stairs to the most ornate suite of offices Vidocq had yet used. The furnishings were elaborate, and everything in the place reeked of money. There was a back entrance for employees, which was also used by clients who didn't want to be seen and by informants.

Vidocq's triumph over his foes was dazzling. The police had bungled so badly they had been humiliated, and a favorite pastime of Paris wits was that of telling new jokes about their ineptitude. The volume of Vidocq's business increased again, until he literally had as many clients as he could handle, and he was forced to ask newcomers to join a waiting list.

His success was not merely the result of the extraordinary publicity he had received. As his customers well knew and told others, he gave them satisfaction. He continued to utilize sound, scientific techniques in his investigations, and his agents were trained, reliable men. The Sûreté was floundering, as writers of newspaper and magazine articles pointed out, because of its failure to adopt Vidocq's approach.

His very success made it easier for him to use informants.

He paid more than the police, he kept confidences, and criminals who came to him ran no risk of arrest. The police could have matched his record only by increasing the size of payments and granting immunity to informants, but they did neither, so it may be — as Vidocq charged — that they didn't understand the principles on which his operation was based.

Among his secret informants were commissaires of police in provincial towns. Experience had taught them that data they had sent the Prefecture in Paris frequently were lost in a sea of red tape, and no action was taken. How much better it was to send information, particularly about swindlers, to Vidocq. Not only were these criminals prosecuted, but the commissaires received handsome cash rewards from the grateful Director of the Information Bureau.

Now at the height of his fame, Vidocq was seen regularly at the theater, and on occasion loaned money to various managers and stars, which was always repaid. His sexual prowess was undiminished, although he was in his late sixties, so he maintained a lively interest in young actresses, almost all of whom, in that era, were part-time courtesans. One with whom his name was linked in the nineteenth century equivalent of gossip columns was the beautiful Lucie Mabire, whom Gautier called the worst actress of the age. She attained stardom because she was lovely, and her sensual appeal crossed the footlights, but managers took care to cast her only in simple roles that required a minimum of histrionic ability. In 1841 Vidocq was seen dining with her on a number of occasions.

The moneylending business continued to boom, too, and Vidocq did not hesitate to sue those who failed to repay his loans. One of them was Prince Charles-Louis de Rohan-Rochefort, one of the leading members of society, who was one of Vidocq's close personal friends. Rohan and his sister, Princess Charlotte, jointly borrowed the very considerable sum of 12,000 francs from Vidocq in 1837 and 1838, and in 1840, when he had not been able to collect a sou from them, he brought a civil action, with Ledru acting as his attorney.

Because of the social prominence of the Rohan-Rocheforts, the case created something of a sensation. The Rohan-Rocheforts denied they were even acquainted with the defendant, but Ledru introduced as evidence more than two hundred friendly letters the Prince had written to Vidocq. In some of them he had begged for money, saying his finances were "desperate." In spite of the evidence against the Prince and Princess, the court ruled in their favor; Ledru promptly appealed, and the higher court reversed the ruling.

This decision was very helpful, Vidocq said in a letter to Ledru, because it convinced other debtors that he would not hesitate to prosecute them, no matter how high their standing in society was, if they failed to repay him. His collection for past debts rose sharply after the Rohan-Rocheforts were forced to send him the full 12,000 francs, along with a 5 per cent penalty imposed by the appellate court.

In 1840 Balzac, who was always in need of money, decided to write a play on Inspector Vautrin, a character he had based on Vidocq. The manager of the Porte Saint-Martin Theatre, one of the leading Paris playhouses, agreed to produce it, and a noted actor, Frédérick Lemaître, was engaged to play the part. Like Vidocq, he was short and powerfully built.

Balzac should not have taken the assignment because he was at work on a novel that required all his time and energy. So, in one of the more celebrated incidents of his colorful life, he turned over the task to five of his friends, asking each of them to write one act.

The result was that *Vautrin* was a confused play of questionable value. Balzac attended the rehearsals, sometimes accompanied by Vidocq, and compounded the madness by making numerous changes. The leading lady became hysterical, and the manager was in despair.

The theater was sold out on the opening night, and Vidocq,

with his wife beside him, was prominent in the audience. Lemaître was magnificent in the title role, but the play itself was a blatant melodrama, with several murders taking part on the stage. Some members of the audience were thrilled, but others walked out. Lemaître was cheered when he appeared for his curtain calls.

Jules Janin, the most influential drama critic of the period, summarized the opinions of his colleagues when he said that he had spent five hours being bored by a work that was inept, desolate and at times barbaric. The play closed after one performance, its demise hastened by the censors, who ruled that in one scene Lemaître was made-up to look like King Louis-Philippe, and that majesty had been mocked.

Vautrin did Vidocq no harm, in spite of its failure. Everybody-who-was-anybody knew the real identity of the central character, and when the censors closed the play the gossip increased.

The production of the play was responsible for one of the more curious incidents in Vidocq's life. Long the gallant escort of aspiring actresses and moneylender to managers and stars, he saw the theater from the inside when he read the script of *Vautrin* and attended its rehearsals, and he loved the experience. It inspired him to write a play of his own, which he appears to have done without the usual aid of professional authors or other ghostwriters.

He completed it in the autumn of 1840 and gave it to an actor friend, La Ferrière, the mainstay of the Vaudeville Theatre, who was one of the biggest stage stars of the period. It was called *Thieves*, and literally nothing is known about it, including La Ferrière's reaction to it. If the actor wrote a critique, it is lost. If the managers of the various theaters with whom Vidocq was well acquainted read and disliked the play, no record of their criticism has survived. The script vanished, the project was abandoned, and Vidocq never mentioned it again. He had other matters on his mind.

Not the least of them was his realization that the police were looking for the chance to strike at him again. Chief of the Sûreté Allard lived in a state of perpetual mortification because the newspapers unfailingly compared his continuing failures with Vidocq's achievements. Then there was the case of Prefect Delessert's brother, Maurice, which made the entire Paris police force a national laughingstock.

Maurice Delessert was a banker whose business establishment was robbed of 75,000 francs, and his brother's men could neither find the thieves nor recover the money. In anger and frustration Delessert wrote to Vidocq for help, using a pseudonym.

Simple detective work revealed his true identity, and Vidocq took personal charge of the case. Using reliable underworld informants he soon learned where the loot was hidden, and made a private deal with the robbers. if they would return the entire sum intact he promised he would not reveal their identity to the authorities, so they would escape prosecution.

Seventy-two hours after he received the appeal for assistance he returned the money to Maurice Delessert, sending it to him under his own name. In a brief accompanying letter he said that he was glad to be of help and, unable to resist the grand gesture, refused to take a fee or commission.

Then, to make matters worse, he sent Prefect Delessert a copy of the communication.

The story was too good to keep, and Vidocq told it to various friends at dinner. Inevitably it leaked out, and soon appeared in the newspapers. Prefect Delessert was deeply embarrassed and, instead of recognizing the ineptitude of the police, was convinced that Vidocq had entered the case only to humiliate him.

One of the younger Sûreté agents, a man whom Vidocq did not know, obtained a position on the Information Bureau staff and was instructed to await the development of a case that would enable the police to hang Vidocq. That opportunity came in August, 1842, soon after the great detective's sixty-seventh birthday.

Early in the summer a clever swindler named Champaix, working through a middleman of small repute who called himself Landier, had obtained credit references from a number of tradesmen amenable to shady deals. Using these references, Champaix bought large quantities of merchandise on credit from honorable merchants, then sold them at a considerable discount to the shady tradesmen.

When the merchants who had been swindled realized what had happened, they went to Vidocq and offered him a considerable percentage of whatever he could recover of their property. The case was routine, offering no unusual problems, and Vidocq handled it as he had scores of others.

First he sent word through the underworld, asking for Champaix's whereabouts, but learned nothing. His second message indicated a willingness to pay for such information. Landier showed up at the Information Bureau, probably using the backstairs, and a bargain was struck.

The following morning Landier led Vidocq and three of his men, among them his chief agent of the time, Gouffé, to a busy street corner. After a short time Champaix appeared and was surrounded, with Vidocq showing him a sheaf of promissory notes he had written but not honored several months earlier, before he had perpetrated his swindle. Under the circumstances Champaix readily agreed to go to the Information Bureau office for a discussion.

There he was subjected to an interrogation that lasted for hours and, before the session ended, he not only signed legally binding papers that would compel him to honor his debts, but he also gave Vidocq a bank draft for several thousand francs, which was all he possessed in cash. Feeling his usual compassion for criminals, Vidocq released him instead of taking him to the police and even gave him five francs so he wouldn't go hungry that night.

The undercover agent went straight to the police with the whole story, and Prefect Delessert believed that here was his chance to ruin Vidocq. The next morning an army of Sûreté agents headed by Allard and a large number of uniformed police under the command of a commissaire appeared at the Information Bureau office. Vidocq and Gouffé were placed under arrest.

They were charged with taking money under false pretenses, making an illegal arrest and kidnaping, apparently the least serious of their alleged offenses. They were taken into custody, given no chance to get in touch with an attorney and taken away.

At noon on August 11, the doors of the Conciergerie closed behind Vidocq. He and Gouffé were lodged in separate cells, each under private guard, and two days passed before they were permitted to get in touch with their wives and lawyers.

This time Prefect Delessert was taking no chances, or so he thought, and believed he had enough evidence to send Vidocq to prison until he died or was so feeble that he would be compelled to retire.

XIV

THE CONCIERGERIE was the oldest, most dilapidated prison
in Paris and was built on the ruins of a jail originally erected
by the Romans, which it incorporated in its structure. As it
was located on the bank of the Seine, water seeped in, making it permanently damp and creating a disagreeable odor
that many people regarded as poisonous. A special commission of inquiry inspected it on behalf of the Ministry of Justice in 1819 and declared it unfit for human habitation, but
the report had been ignored and the prison was still in use
twenty-three years later. Overcrowded and unsanitary, with
dripping walls and filled with a stench that often made visitors ill, it was called the hellhole by its inmates.

On August 23 Mme. Vidocq sent a short note to the Prefect, requesting permission to see her husband and remark-
ing that "at his advanced age he needs care and comfort."
The request was denied.

On September 1 Charles Ledru wrote to the Prefect, demanding that his client be moved to a jail less harmful to his
health. The request was denied.

On October 2 Vidocq himself wrote to the Prefect, declar-
ing that the dampness of the Conciergerie was causing him
"attacks of catarrh and rheumatism." Delessert appointed a
physician to examine him, and the doctor reported that the
prisoner was enjoying robust health. The request was
denied.

On October 19 Vidocq wrote again to the Prefect, asking for permission to receive visits from his wife in his cell. He could not see her in the visitors' room, he said, because other prisoners had access to it, and one or another of them might try to kill him. The request was denied.

When Charles Ledru came to see his client and friend late in October, he found Vidocq in a dangerous frame of mind. Rather than tolerate further police harassment, he declared, he would send his wife to another country, carrying the better part of their convertible assets, and he would join her there. How would he accomplish this feat? He would escape, of course, just as he had done so many times in his youth. No prison could hold Vidocq once he made up his mind to get out.

Ledru made a point of repeating the conversation in certain circles in order to make certain it made its way back to the Prefect. Delessert was vindictive, but had enough intelligence to realize he would be laughed out of office if Vidocq made good his threat, which he was capable of doing. So the prisoner's confinement was eased. He was given a large, relatively dry cell facing inland, his wife was permitted to visit him in his cell and so were his legal representatives.

Meanwhile the police were doing a thorough job of ruining the Information Bureau. They ransacked the offices, wantonly destroying files and confiscating thousands of documents irrelevant to the charges against Vidocq. Expensive furniture and rugs vanished. Many employees were browbeaten into submitting their resignations, and even the bureau's nameplate was removed from the front door.

Vidocq could do nothing to halt these outrages, and Ledru protested in vain. In fact, late in 1842, Ledru reached the conclusion that it would be unwise for him to act as the defendant's principal attorney. The government was becoming increasingly reactionary as Louis-Philippe displayed more and more short-sighted Bourbon tendencies, and Ledru was unpopular at the Ministry of Justice because of his outspoken republican convictions.

So he engaged the only advocate in France he regarded as his peer, selflessly reducing himself to the role of an anonymous assistant. Jules Favre was a brilliant attorney, an exceptionally effective speaker and, like Ledru, he believed passionately that the cause of justice had to be served or society would perish.

The police found it so difficult to substantiate the charges they had brought against Vidocq that the Court of Assizes refused to hear the case, a panel of three jurists ruling that the evidence was lacking. So the Prefect persuaded the President of the Police Court, Michel Barbou, to hear the case. This judge knew Vidocq by reputation, but had never met him in person, so it was assumed he would be fair, even though his association with the Prefect was close. Ledru and Favre believed he had a limited understanding of the law.

The trial opened on May 3, 1843, and that morning Vidocq left the Conciergerie for the first time since his imprisonment the previous August. The courtroom was crowded with members of the French and foreign press, most of whom noted that his face was deeply lined and that he looked "ravaged." Several wrote in wonder, however, that he had no gray hair, and it did not occur to them that he might have used dye or worn a wig. He was expensively dressed in black and he bowed, smiled and waved to his friends as he entered.

The prosecutor, in his opening statement, made it plain that Champaix would be a principal witness for the state. He claimed that Vidocq had arrested him "in the name of the law," and had searched him thoroughly after taking him against his will to the Information Bureau office. It was clear to the defense from the outset that Champaix had been promised immunity from prosecution in return for telling this story.

The first witness called to the stand was Vidocq himself, and under Magistrate Barbou's questioning he recounted his entire career, proudly digressing to describe his forgery-proof paper and ink and to explain the philosophy that had led him to hire former criminals at his paper-box factory.

Occasionally he showed flashes of fire, as he did when the judge asked "Were you not in fact dismissed from the Sûreté?"

"Never!" Vidocq retorted. "I myself placed my voluntary resignation on file at the Ministry."

"Why is it not filed at the Prefecture since you were in the direct employ of the police?"

"Mr. President," Vidocq said, "I feel certain everyone in this courtroom knows I have no cause to trust the police. If my resignation had been filed at the Prefecture they could have destroyed it and substituted a false order saying I had been discharged."

"You think, then, they are as untrustworthy as criminals?"

Vidocq smiled. "That, sir, is a question I prefer not to contemplate."

Eventually the court dealt with the specific nature of the charges against Vidocq. In answer to Magistrate Barbou's questions, Vidocq denied he had masqueraded as a police officer when approaching Champaix, he insisted the swindler was not held in isolation or against his will at the Information Bureau office, and he vigorously denied that he had stolen money from Champaix.

A former Information Bureau agent, one Ulisse Perronoud, was called to the stand and denied every statement made by Vidocq and by Gouffé, whose story had echoed that of his superior. They had pretended to be policemen, they had held Champaix under close guard at their office, and they had browbeaten him until he had paid them a portion of the money he had obtained by legal means from their clients.

Magistrate Barbou remarked that the mere mention of Vidocq's name was sufficient to paralyze a criminal.

The defense tried to prove that Perronoud was actually a police spy, that he had obtained a position at the Information

Bureau for the purpose of trapping Vidocq and, above all, that his testimony was a series of lies. Perronoud denied that he worked for the police and insisted he was telling the truth.

A tavern owner and several of her clients testified that Perronoud really was in the employ of the police as an undercover agent, and that he had boasted about his real job when drinking with them. Several other witnesses said the same thing.

The case presented by the prosecution depended on the reliability of Perronoud's word. But Magistrate Barbou elected not to pursue the matter and instead demanded to know whether certain other stories about Vidocq were valid. Was it true that he had been responsible for the abduction of two young ladies from the Convent of Saint-Michel?

Vidocq returned to the stand and obligingly explained both cases. In one, the parents of a girl not yet of age came to him for help in breaking up her romance with a fortune hunter. Vidocq had met the girl, but she had refused to accept his word that her lover was a notorious procurer. Her parents had taken her to the convent, and Vidocq had accompanied the family on that occasion. Two weeks later the girl had escaped, and since that time had been living openly with her lover. Furthermore she had found employment as an "actress," and was supporting herself and her lover by sleeping with men whom she met at the theater. Her parents had realized she was incorrigible and had disowned her.

The second case was far more pleasant. A young woman who had two small children had fled from the home of a husband who had beaten and abused her. Ultimately she had found a new home with a gentle and generous lover who had given the family a good home, wanted to marry the woman and adopt her children.

One day she had spent too much of her lover's money on a shopping spree, and her guilt had so overwhelmed her that she had gone to the Convent of Saint-Michel and had taken refuge there. When she had failed to return home her lover had been alarmed, and had engaged the Information Bureau to find her.

Vidocq had located her within twenty-four hours, and this was the only part he had played in the matter. The lover had gone to the convent, a reconciliation had taken place and the couple had remained together since that time.

The attempts to blacken Vidocq's name having failed, other efforts were made, with Magistrate Barbou making most of the accusations. It was true, was it not, that Vidocq had abducted a young woman on behalf of a client and turned her over to him?

The defense called the young lady to the stand. Now happily married to someone else, she testified that Vidocq had not only rejected the request of her former suitor, but had come to her and warned her of the man's intentions. Thereafter she had been guarded by Information Bureau agents for several weeks, and Vidocq had refused to accept a sou in return.

Eight other cases were recalled, and a parade of defense witnesses refuted a variety of charges against Vidocq. The prosecution was finding it impossible to present him as a villain.

The courtroom spectators were amused by the details of one case, in which the prosecution claimed that Vidocq was as big a swindler as the men he exposed. A nobleman who lived in the provinces and rarely came to Paris, the Marquis du Vivier, enjoyed being a large fish in a small pond but wanted to be more important. For years he had yearned for the award of membership in the Legion of Honor but had done nothing to earn such a place.

He had come to Paris to enlist the aid of Vidocq but had been told there was nothing the detective could do for him. The Legion of Honor was given for distinguished service in any one of a number of fields of endeavor and it couldn't be bought.

The Marquis absorbed the information, went home and pondered for several months. Then he wrote to Vidocq and said he felt certain it would be possible to arrange for the award of foreign decorations. Vidocq tried to persuade him to forget the idea, and copies of his letters were introduced as evidence.

But the Marquis badly wanted to appear in public wearing bits of brightly colored ribbon on his chest and could not be dissuaded. Finally, with no encouragement from Vidocq, he sent the Information Bureau a bank draft for 3000 francs and demanded that something be done for him.

So Vidocq, hoping to be rid of him, went to a dealer who sold old coins and decorations, and arranged to have two medals in solid gold made up for the Marquis. Accompanying them were engraved certificates of membership in orders that Vidocq invented for the purpose. He had to spend 2800 of du Vivier's 3000 francs for the false decorations and certificates, and the agent who took the "awards" to the Marquis incurred expenses of one hundred francs. This left a profit of one hundred francs, and Vidocq said he had been forced to spend so much time dealing with the absurd matter that he had actually lost money.

Now that the affair had come into the open the Marquis was deeply embarrassed. When summoned as a witness, he insisted he no longer wanted the medals and ribbons. When examined by Magistrate Barbou he refused to implicate Vidocq or admit he had been cheated.

The prosecution nevertheless insisted that Vidocq had swindled him. No one in the courtroom — with the exception of Magistrate Barbou — took the matter seriously.

A parade of witnesses testified in Vidocq's favor, including several members of the bench. Among them was the retired former Presiding Magistrate of Paris, Arnold De Bernis, one of the most distinguished of living judges. Procurator General Franck-Carré again testified for Vidocq, and told of an incident that had taken place in 1839, when a band of rioters had intended to attack him at his home. Vidocq had learned of their intentions and had driven them off; he had not even mentioned the matter to the Procurator General, and many months had passed before Franck-Carré had learned that Vidocq had saved his life.

On June 17, after a trial that had lasted for a month and a half, the court rendered its verdict. Vidocq was found guilty of illegally placing Champaix under arrest and seizing his money. He was also found guilty of fraud in the case of the Marquis du Vivier.

The defendant was sentenced to a term of five years in prison and was fined 3000 francs.

Even the police, the reporters attending the trial wrote, were shocked by the severity of the sentence. Vidocq's conduct, they said, was superb. His face betraying no emotion, he bowed to the Presiding Magistrate Barbou and withdrew from the courtroom without speaking a word.

Jules Favre and Charles Ledru had no intention of accepting the verdict, and that same day they appealed the case to the higher court. They were joined in their strategy sessions by retired Magistrate de Bernis and, unofficially, by Procurator General Franck-Carré. Then they brought in the most eloquent of their colleagues, Jean Landrin, to present the case before the Court of Appeals.

Vidocq, who had been returned to his cell, wrote a long and impassioned memorandum defending himself, then had it printed and distributed free of charge to the public. This document had no influence on the case.

Presiding Justice Michel Simonneau decided to hear the appeal himself and was flanked by two other justices on July 22, 1843. The trial lasted only two days, members of the court having already familiarized themselves with the details of the case.

Advocate Landrin was crisp and firm on Vidocq's behalf but on the second day of the hearing he gave in to emotion and launched an attack on Champaix, the swindler. Justice

Simonneau halted him and informed him that he had already established his case on Vidocq's behalf.

The traditional recess taken so the justices could confer and vote was brief. The Court of Appeals ruled that Vidocq had been acting within the law on behalf of Champaix's legitimate creditors and was guilty neither of false arrest nor the taking of money from Champaix. As for the ridiculous case of the Marquis du Vivier, the court dryly observed that, in view of the time and effort Vidocq had expended, the profit he had earned had been far too small.

Vidocq was a free man after spending almost a year in prison, and Procurator General Franck-Carré personally signed the order releasing him.

The offices in the Galerie Vivienne were reopened the following day, and Paris was filled with posters that shouted: **RESURRECTION! Hatred of Rogues! Boundless Devotion to Trade!**

The sixty-eight-year-old Vidocq courageously tried to revive his business, but the task was overwhelming. His legal fees for himself and Gouffé were large, he had to replace furniture that had been smashed or carted away by unknown persons. Even more important, he had to hire a new staff and painstakingly rebuild the files that had been rifled and destroyed.

Many loyal clients returned to him, but others hesitated. His files had been seized on two separate occasions within recent years, and some people didn't want the police prying into their private business.

Vidocq persisted, however, and showed his customary energy that months of imprisonment had not diminished. For two months he worked day and night, even establishing living quarters for himself in the office suite so that he would lose no time in going to and from an apartment. Mme. Vidocq had been frugal during his absence, and he was still a fairly wealthy man, so he was prepared to do anything necessary to restore the Information Bureau to its former glory.

But the police were not yet finished with him. Prefect Delessert had been conferring with his own attorneys, and an old law that had never been rescinded was revived for Vidocq's benefit. On September 22, 1843, Vidocq was served with a formal Order of the Prefect. Twice, the document stated, he had been tried on serious criminal charges, but no mention was made of his acquittal. Further, he had been sentenced to the galleys in 1796; the Order neglected to state that he had been pardoned for the crime he had committed in his youth. The document also ignored the fact that he had served as a high-ranking police officer for many years.

Vidocq was banned from Paris and would be required to establish a residence in exile somewhere in the provinces. The communication ended on an ominous note:

> We command the said Vidocq to present himself at the Prefecture of Police, 1st Bureau, in order to receive a passport to the residence he considers he should choose.
>
> In the event that he does not comply with this injunction, he will be prosecuted according to the law.

Vidocq was not intimidated and had no intention of obeying an order obviously intended to harass him. He announced that he would fight, regardless of the outcome.

His friends immediately rallied to his cause, and a meeting was held in the office of Pierre Bonjean, Principal Advocate of the Court of Appeals. Among those in attendance were Ledru, Landrin, Favre, Magistrate de Bernis and Procurator General Franck-Carré. It was their considered opinion that the order was invalid and illegal, and they issued a public memorandum to that effect, saying that they were advising Vidocq to ignore it.

Prefect Delessert had no intention of backing down, however, and made plans to take the issue to court. Apparently his own legal advisers were assuring him that he would win. If Vidocq was served with a court summons it meant he would necessarily be prosecuted by one of Franck-Carré's assistants, and the Procurator General decided to intervene. He sent a firm letter to Prefect Delessert in which he pulled no punches:

1. Vidocq had just been acquitted by the Court of Appeals after a trial that had aroused the interest of the entire country.

2. The tide of public opinion ran heavily in Vidocq's favor, and the people of France would regard his further prosecution as persecution.

3. Any actions taken against Vidocq without specific, due cause would be in bad taste and would offend public morality, thus adding to the lack of popularity the police already were suffering.

4. Some of the nation's leading lawyers held the unanimous opinion that the Order of the Prefect was illegal and could not be enforced.

5. The Procurator General agreed with this opinion, and consequently would permit no prosecutor in the employ of the Ministry of Justice to represent the police in any proceedings the Prefect might wish to undertake.

Delessert had to concede defeat. Never had it been necessary for the police to hire an outside prosecutor to represent them in a case, and the refusal of the Ministry of Justice to cooperate with him meant he could not win. The Order of the Prefect was quietly withdrawn.

Vidocq announced his victory to the press but took care not to gloat. He knew it would be virtually impossible for the police to attack or harass him again and he was willing to let the entire matter drop. All he wanted was the right to live the rest of his life as he wished, in the public eye.

XV

THE NEXT TWO YEARS were among the most pleasant and harmonious of Vidocq's long life. His attempts to revitalize the Information Bureau were only partly successful, but as he approached seventy such things were not as important as they had been. He was renowned, universally respected, and he no longer felt compelled to prove himself to the public. He received more dinner invitations from people of stature than he could possibly accept, and the great men of the era were proud to be seen in his company. Vidocq was satisfied.

His wife had been weakened by the strains of recent years and retired more or less permanently to the country house in Saint-Mandé. Vidocq joined her there for weekends and holidays, allowing no other engagements to interfere. In his own way he was devoted to Fleuride.

He modified his habits, no longer venturing into the underworld in disguise, permitting young agents in his employ to conduct strenuous surveillances. His physical strength was undiminished, as he frequently told the flabby Balzac who was irritated by these boasts, but his stamina appeared to be declining. Nevertheless he spent long days in his office, seeing clients and supervising investigations, and he slept in his apartment behind the Information Bureau on the infrequent occasions when more promising opportunities failed to arise.

He rarely dined alone and was an honored guest at restaurant parties or the homes of friends who never tired of listening to the innumerable stories of his exploits. Late in the evenings he devoted himself to young actresses, shopgirls and models. Hugo, who was equally indefatigable in his pursuit of beauty, admired Vidocq's taste and praised his stamina. When a pretty girl entered a public place Vidocq unfailingly observed her, and he appeared to be endowed with a sixth sense that told him when a woman was available.

In his seventieth year, according to the awed Balzac, he had as many as three mistresses at the same time, spending a night with each in turn. He rarely paid for the favors of his companions but had the knack of convincing each that he was in love with her. When he gave them gifts he presented them with inexpensive bottles of perfume or silver earrings that he bought from a friendly jeweler at less than the retail price. Presumably he was given a wholesale rate because he bought these items in bulk.

Vidocq again busied himself as an author, or at least published books that appeared under his name. The first of these, *Quelques Mots*, which appeared in 1844, was a revised version of *Les Voleurs*. In it he resumed his arguments in favor of the rehabilitation of released prisoners, and he devoted the entire proceeds of the sale of the work to a colony of ex-convicts that had been established on a large farm about seventy-five miles from Paris.

Late in 1844 Vidocq published a novel. Taking advantage of the success of Eugène Sue's *Les Mystères de Paris*, he blithely called his book *Les Vrais Mystères de Paris*. It was a huge work, published in seven volumes and sold for the whopping price of forty-five francs.

The material, which dealt with criminals, their way of life and their professional techniques, could have been supplied by no one but Vidocq himself. Some of the characters, obviously taken from real life, could be recognized, and the work was encyclopedic in scope. It should have been required reading for the police because the crime rate was rising again.

Vidocq is known to have given his original notes and other material to Horace Raisson, the author of two inferior histories of the Paris police, who had recently become a novelist. How much work Raisson did on the *Vrais Mystères* cannot be ascertained, but the results did not satisfy Vidocq, who took the project away from his collaborator. Several years later Raisson published his version under the original title, *Une Sombre Histoire*, under the pseudonym of Mortonval, but the stories and incidents were so similar to the material in Vidocq's work that few readers bought the book.

As was to be expected, Vidocq claimed that he rewrote his novel himself, but that is unlikely. It is probable that the actual author was Alfred Lucas, who was again in his employ. The style was too smooth, the writing too crisp for Vidocq to have done it himself. In any event the *Vrais Mystères* was a success, selling more than 20,000 copies, and for the rest of the nineteenth century the writers of increasingly popular detective fiction used incidents from the novel as source material.

Some of Vidocq's characters were insufficiently disguised. The proprietor of a restaurant in the Passage de l'Opéra, the Divan, filed suit for slander because his establishment was described as a criminal hangout, and he himself appeared as a receiver of stolen goods. Vidocq was represented by Landrin, but even that distinguished attorney could not persuade the court that any resemblance between the restaurant owner and the character in the book was purely coincidental. Vidocq had to pay damages of five hundred francs and court costs.

The proprietor of a shop in the rue Planche-Mibray, a man named Lauvergnat, also filed a slander suit against Vidocq, but this time Landrin was more persuasive. The suit was settled out of court for twenty-five francs, Lauvergnat obviously having been more interested in the restoration of his honor than in cash.

The second of Vidocq's novels was called *Les Chauffeurs du Nord,* and appeared under the imprint of a popular publishing firm, Comon. It was published in five volumes, two of them printed in 1845, and the remaining three in 1846.

According to some sources the actual author was one Auguste Vitu, a writer who specialized in doing books for others, and who received a police appointment as a sub-prefect several years later. The style was ornate and convoluted and bore little resemblance to the sentences and paragraphs that appeared in the *Vrais Mystères.*

Again, only Vidocq could have supplied the material. The story concerned the dreaded highwaymen who had terrorized northern France during the Revolution, murdering, torturing and robbing wantonly. Vidocq had known a number of such bands at precisely that period, when he had been on the run from the authorities after his many escapes from custody.

Long sections of the book deal with the galleys, and both living conditions and the inmates are described in pinpoint detail. Vidocq, with his extraordinary memory, well remembered his own experiences in the galleys.

Only the elderly knew that *Les Chauffeurs* dealt with real men and actual living conditions that had existed more than a half-century earlier. Younger generations thought Vidocq had dipped into his imagination for a horror story about vicious criminals. In any event, readers old and young were thrilled, and even though the book cost thirty-eight francs more than 30,000 copies were sold; the highwaymen of the North became permanent fixtures in French detective fiction.

In both novels Vidocq lost no opportunity to write scathingly of the police under Prefect Delessert and the weakened Sûreté directed by Allard. There was no comparison between the uniformed police and the detective bureau commanded by these dullards and the splendid forces that had protected Parisians two decades earlier, he said. He took care not to present his enemies in person, either as themselves or disguised, as he knew Delessert and Allard would be delighted to sue him for libel. But that did not prevent his characters from talking about them at length and presenting them in the worst possible light.

By this time the police were sick of Vidocq and had no desire to tangle with him again. No matter how much Delessert and Allard may have been angered by his harsh, goading criticism, they had the good sense to say nothing in public and to take no action against the author of the *Vrais Mystères* and the *Chauffeurs*.

The time was not yet ripe for the reorganization of the police and the reformation of the Sûreté, and Vidocq, who would have relished being placed in charge of the overhaul, made no overt moves to win such an appointment. The increasingly reactionary acts and attitudes displayed by the government of Louis-Philippe were creating a more strident demand for the establishment of a republic. Vidocq, who had lived through so many violent upheavals, remarked at dinner to Charles Ledru that Parisians would erect street barricades again, and only then would the police — and especially the Sûreté — be placed on a sound footing.

Late in 1845 Ledru was the principal speaker at a dinner given in honor of a retiring justice of the Court of Appeals, and among the guests were other members of the bench, high-ranking officials of the Ministry of Justice and several police officials. Never one to remain silent or avoid controversy, Ledru utilized the occasion to call for a return to "the time of Vidocq" at the Sûreté. It would be presumptuous to ask the old warrior to undertake the enormous task himself, he declared, then wondered aloud whether there were any younger men in France who had Vidocq's dedication to duty, courage and knowledge of the criminal mind. He was given a standing ovation.

In his *Mémoires* Ledru claims that a number of the younger Sûreté agents agreed with him, and came to him privately to congratulate him. They could not protest aloud without losing their jobs but they felt the Sûreté was moribund. The problem, the lawyer declared in his *Mémoires*, was that the Sûreté continued to work in secret, so the general public failed to realize how ineffective the bureau had become.

Certainly by the early 1840's the seeds sown by Vidocq were taking root elsewhere, and the idea of establishing police bureaus of criminal investigation, with some agents in civilian clothes, was beginning to spread. It is not coincidental that in April, 1841, *Graham's Magazine* in Philadelphia published a short story by Edgar Allan Poe, *The Murders in the Rue Morgue*, often called the world's most perfect detective story. Poe freely admitted he had read and been influenced by Vidocq's *Mémoires*, and that he had set his scene in the underworld of Vidocq's Paris.

There was one essential difference between the written works of the two men, apart from their literary values or lack of them. The hero of Vidocq's books, regardless of whether they were non-fiction or fiction, was always Vidocq, the professional detective. Poe established a different tradition that has provided the core of most detective fiction written for more than a century. His protagonist was the analytical, levelheaded amateur, the outsider who used his intellectual powers to solve cases.

Poe's story proved so popular that he wrote others in the same vein, but more than a decade would pass before the principle became reality. The New York Police established a detective bureau in 1854, and six men were assigned to it for the "investigation of crimes of passion." The experiment proved so successful that the bureau was expanded, and before the outbreak of the Civil War in 1861, approximately one hundred American cities and town had subdivisions employing plainclothes detectives for the investigation of crimes.

Great Britain acted more quickly. In fact, the so-called Bow

Street Runners performed a few basic police functions on behalf of the judges of the Bow Street courts in the mid-eighteenth century. Their basic task was that of arresting criminals for whom warrants had been issued.

The real history of the modern police in Britain began in 1829, when Sir Robert Peel founded a force of men who bore blue uniforms. They made their headquarters in a compound located in Scotland Yard, and from the outset the force was known by that name. "Bobbies," as the police came to be called, met violent public opposition in their early years, but the hostilities faded gradually.

The top-ranking officials of Scotland Yard showed a great interest in the Sûreté, and in 1832 a committee composed of three senior officers visited Paris and spent several days with Vidocq. His *Mémoires*, which were published in a translation in London in 1830, were widely read, but not until seven years later did a special police commission start work on the possible formation of a detective bureau.

The work progressed slowly in London, due in part to the continuing hatred the public had for the police, most opposition being based on the supposition that the men in blue would try to curtail the personal liberties of which Englishmen were justly proud. So experiments were conducted with caution, the government not wanting to create a public furor, and the Criminal Investigation Department of Scotland Yard was not formally organized until 1842.

It was modeled closely on the Brigade de la Sûreté to the extent that its detectives wore civilian clothes most of the time, utilized the latest scientific techniques in their work and used the services of paid informants. But there was one major difference between the Scotland Yard force and the Sûreté. All members of the Criminal Investigation Department were full-time, salaried employees, police officers who had started their careers in uniform and had come up through the ranks. The grade of detective was higher than that of the policeman on patrol duty. No bonuses or fees of any kind were paid for arrests, convictions or any other duties performed.

The Department was headed by a senior inspector, who was aided by a junior inspector, and under them were six sergeants and eleven detectives. They worked out of a small suite in a corner of the Scotland Yard compound and initially they were treated with the same scorn by their colleagues that the Sûreté had encountered since Vidocq had founded it.

The Criminal Investigation Department scored a number of solid successes in its first months of existence, and after five members of a gang of robbers were captured late in 1842, opposition to it within the uniformed ranks began to fade. Soon the detectives were recognized by their colleagues as members of an elite band, and the inspector in charge was inundated with requests for transfers to the new organization. From the time of the founding of the Department a firm policy was established: a policeman's record was the only factor taken into account, and promotions to the grade of detective were made exclusively on the basis of merit.

Late in 1843, after Vidocq's release from prison, the two Scotland Yard inspectors paid a visit to Paris, ostensibly to see Allard and study the operations of the Brigade de la Sûreté. Apparently they were not impressed because they spent only two days with him, devoting most of that time to courtesy calls on the Prefect and other officials. Then they appeared at the offices of the Information Bureau in the Galerie Vivienne.

For the next week they listened to Vidocq, watched him at work, interviewed his agents and examined his laboratory. They realized, of course, that they were dealing with the founder of their profession, and Vidocq, who loved a responsive audience, took them into his confidence. The visitors were even accorded the unusual honor of spending a few days with Vidocq and his wife at Saint-Mandé. After the pair returned to London the *Times* noted in a small article that

Vidocq had taught them "many tricks of the trade." Readers were told no details.

Before leaving Paris the Englishmen returned Vidocq's generous hospitality by inviting him to visit London at his convenience.

He had known the Low Countries in his youth but had never traveled for pleasure, and, for all practical purposes, had spent his entire life in France. So the idea of going to England strongly appealed to him. He was well known there, thanks in part to the translation of his *Mémoires* and the play loosely based on it, and also because the London press frequently published articles about his activities. So he felt certain he would be given a warm welcome.

But the re-creation of the Information Bureau after his imprisonment was a task that occupied his energies for the next two years, and in his spare time he worked with his collaborators on his books. Not until the late autumn of 1845, after the publication of the first two volumes of the *Chauffeurs*, was he free to make the journey.

In spite of his efforts the Information Bureau had not regained its previous eminence, and although the modest operation was still profitable it was no longer exciting. Vidocq may have been glad to let his senior agents supervise investigations while Mme. Vidocq took care of the accounts. She also kept watch on the sales of his book, and he gave her full powers of attorney to deal with his business affairs as she saw fit during his absence.

His command of English was adequate, and he was still so quick-witted he felt confident he would soon become even more fluent in the foreign tongue. He took a large sum of money with him, carefully exchanging some hundreds of francs into pounds before his departure, and he booked his passage in advance.

Late in the autumn of 1845 the seventy-year-old Vidocq sailed from Boulogne on a new adventure.

XVI

LONDON IN THE 1840's was the fastest-growing city in the Old World. The Industrial Revolution had started in England, and the combination of natural resources, ample power and cheap labor were responsible for a remarkable rate of growth. Factories that manufactured both capital and consumer goods were being built everywhere, the British Empire was still expanding, the Royal Navy was the undisputed mistress of the seas and the growing middle class was accumulating great wealth.

New hotels, restaurants and theaters, tailoring establishments, purveyors of fine foods and brothels were mushrooming, and the population of London had doubled since the end of the Napoleonic Wars. According to some estimates, almost two million people now made their home in the bustling metropolis. Stately new government buildings and handsome mansions were being erected at so rapid a rate that entire neighborhoods were being transformed, and it did not matter to most men in positions of authority that the poor were more miserable, more downtrodden than ever before. Only Scotland Yard was interested in the inevitable surge in the crime rate.

Vidocq, who was regarded by the English as something of an enigma because he had been portrayed by the press as a mysterious, rather sinister person, entered the maelstrom with innocent, high hopes. He intended to call on his colleagues at Scotland Yard, to be sure, but he was their teacher, and there was little they could do for him.

He entertained many new ambitions, all of them commercial. He intended to hold meetings with a minor writer, Frederick Tolfrey, with whom he had been corresponding and who wanted to translate some of his books into English. He hoped to lease his paper and ink patents to English manufacturers and was relying on the assistance of a fellow countryman, Stéphane Etiévant, who had already visited a number of paper companies on his behalf. He was thinking of writing yet another book of memoirs and offering them to London publishers for initial publication. And it so happened that he carried with him several trunks filled with criminals' tools and weapons, forging equipment, disguises that he had worn and paintings that illustrated various phases of his career. He intended, if he could, to open an exhibit and show these mementos to the public, for a fee. He also wanted to explore the possibility of opening a branch of the Information Bureau in London.

Vidocq engaged a second-floor suite at 207, Regent Street, a building in which a tavern was conveniently located on the ground floor. He sent cordial notes to the newspapers, inviting their representatives to call on him and for a week he entertained reporters in the tavern, answering their questions and telling stories about clever criminals he had outwitted. The response was gratifying, the newspapers running long columns about the great French master detective. Now Vidocq was in a position to launch the various projects that had brought him across the Channel.

Overnight he encountered unexpected obstacles. The first was the discovery that Etiévant and his wife were languishing in a debtors' prison and were totally without funds. He alone knew the paper and ink manufacturers Vidocq wanted to interest in his patents. Frederick Tolfrey, the translator, was in a slightly less desperate situation, but prison beckoned. He owed his landlord for back rent, had accumulated a number of other debts and was penniless.

Had Vidocq been in Paris he would have looked elsewhere for help, but he knew no one else in huge, bewildering London, and he believed he needed the assistance of his bankrupt acquaintances. So he bailed Etiévant and his wife out of jail, giving them enough money to pay their living expenses for a time, and was equally generous with Tolfrey. Presumably they were now prepared to go to work on his behalf.

Vidocq entered protracted negotiations with a publisher named Newby, who had offices at 72, Mortimer Street, Cavendish Square. They agreed that Vidocq would write a new book of memoirs, to be published in six volumes, which would be translated into English and would first appear in London. Vidocq would receive seventy pounds per volume for the first edition and one hundred and seventeen pounds per volume for each succeeding edition.

The negotiations hit a snag when Vidocq insisted that the memoirs be serialized before publication in book form. Newby demurred, believing that the appearance of all or part of the work in the newspapers would detract from the sale of his edition. Both men were stubborn and held firm, with each hoping the other would give way.

Meanwhile Etiévant, who was still being supported by his reluctant benefactor, was singularly unsuccessful in his alleged attempts to arrange deals with English paper and ink manufacturers. Vidocq suspected that he was drinking heavily and paying little attention to business. Tolfrey was proving to be a drain, too, requesting money every week and sulking when he wasn't given as much as he wanted and thought he deserved, even though he had not yet translated a line.

In the midst of these troubles Vidocq opened his exhibition in quarters he rented near his lodgings on Regent Street. It was a curious jumble consisting of three sections that bore little or no relation to each other.

The first part was an exhibition of paintings from Vidocq's own collection. According to the newspaper accounts the place of honor was given to watercolors by a Dutch artist, Dirk Langendyk, most of them battle scenes in the Low Countries during the early years of the French Revolution. Vidocq, to be sure, had fought in some of these engagements.

Other artists represented included Philip Wouwerman, Albert Cuyp and Peter van Laar. There were a number of paintings, too, by French and Italian artists whom the newspapers did not bother to name. Some paintings were of landscapes, a few were portraits of people unknown in England, and a handful portrayed criminals at work, the one subject that fascinated Londoners.

The second portion of the exhibition can only be described as strange. It consisted of wax models of tropical fruits, originally intended by its makers to be presented as a gift to King Louis-Philippe. Vidocq did not explain how they had come into his possession. These models were of sixty varieties, and more than 4000 individual specimens were laid out on long tables.

The third part of the exhibit was made up of items the public truly wanted to see. Here were row after row of knives, pistols and hooks used by murderers Vidocq had captured. There was the innocent-looking rope of braided silk that a strangler had used to do away with five victims. In a place of honor was a phial supposedly containing poison that Vidocq had correctly identified and, armed with these data, had captured yet another killer.

The *Times* called the exhibition "gruesome," and with good cause. There were scores of instruments of torture, some dating from the Middle Ages, others of more modern manufacture. There was the frock coat worn by a murderer who had gone to the guillotine, and the spots that stained its collar were self-explanatory. In a special place were chains and leaded boots worn by convicts in the galleys, and nearby were the leaded whips used by their guards.

Other items were somewhat less gory. There were samples of forged papers and signatures of the famous, false stock certificates, the counterfeit paper money and coins of many nations and decks of marked playing cards. Since the beginning of his career Vidocq had been collecting these souvenirs, and now they were gathered in one place.

The price of admission was five shillings, which would have been excessive for a collection of paintings, wax fruit and criminals' tools, but Vidocq gave his customers their money's worth. Twice daily he appeared in person on a small, makeshift stage, first making several rapid changes from one disguise to another, then delivering a lecture that was complete with anecdotes about himself.

The reaction of the *Times* to his extraordinary little show was typically poised:

> The principal curiosity in the collection will prove to be M. Vidocq himself, whose appearance is very much what might be anticipated. He is a remarkably well-built man, of exceptional muscular power, and exceedingly active. He stands, when perfectly erect, perhaps five feet ten inches in height, but by some strange process connected with his physical formation he has the faculty of contracting his height several inches, and in this diminished state to walk about, jump, etc.
>
> His countenance exhibits, in a way not to be mistaken, unflinching determination of character, strong powers of perception and that bluffness which denotes animal courage. He is extremely intelligent, good-humored and communicative. From the flexibility of his features, and his powers of varying the expression of them, he would make an excellent player in such representations as require an actor to sustain several parts.
>
> He is now seventy-two years of age [sic], but possesses all the strength, vigour and bouyancy of a man twenty-five years his junior. Those who admire the marvellous and wish to witness its illustration will be gratified by this exhibition.

Visitors to the exhibit were also presented with a free gift, a brochure entitled *Vidocq, Chef de la Police de Sûreté (Detective Force) de Paris, Which Was Created by Him, and*

Which He Directed for Twenty-nine Years [sic] *with Extraordinary Success.* This booklet, which was autographed by Vidocq, included a colorful, exaggerated account of his exploits and a catalogue of the objects on display in the exhibit. At the back was an advertisement for the forthcoming six-volume memoirs. The author of the pamphlet was not identified, but may have been Tolfrey.

Only one publication attacked the show and its star. A critic named Williams, writing in the *Weekly Dispatch*, called Vidocq a charlatan and urged the Home Secretary to close the exhibit before Anglo-French relations were permanently harmed. Other publications, including the influential *Era*, immediately came to Vidocq's defense.

The old lion needed no one's help, and wrote a blistering letter to the editors of the *Weekly Dispatch*, which the *Era* obligingly printed, in which he called them "infamous calumniators, odious liars with a base and malevolent spirit." He also promised to thrash the editors, separately or jointly, at any time he might encounter them.

The editors of the *Weekly Dispatch* were afraid Vidocq meant his threat to be taken seriously, and they printed a warning that they would take him to court if he attacked them. They also hired bodyguards to protect them from this ferocious foreigner.

The furor, which was duly reported by the daily newspapers, did Vidocq's exhibit in Regent Street no harm, and the hall was filled for both of his performances each day. The show lasted a little more than five months. Vidocq, who enjoyed his luxuries, used twenty pounds per week for his living expenses and dutifully sent his wife about one hundred pounds per week.

Undoubtedly he spent some of his money entertaining actresses and other young women about town. He was seen at supper with one or another beauty regularly, so it is obvious that neither advancing age nor a language barrier altered his habits of a lifetime.

His attempts to establish a branch of the Information Bureau in London were not successful, perhaps because the time was not yet ripe there for the creation of a private detective agency. But he did manage to help Scotland Yard bring a swindler to justice. One of his clients in Antwerp had been cheated by a criminal named Jean Diemer, whom Vidocq had sent to prison some years earlier. The client wrote to Vidocq, saying he understood Diemer was now in London. Going to work on his own initiative, Vidocq set up his own contacts in the London underworld and soon located Diemer. Then he called in Scotland Yard to make the arrest and, with uncharacteristic modesty, refused to take any credit for his part in the exploit.

When the exhibit closed Vidocq returned to Paris for a short time, then went back to England for the purpose of enjoying himself. He had no business to occupy him there any longer, so he went sightseeing, attended the theater regularly and became very friendly with a Mme. Céleste, the manager-star of the Adelphi Theatre. Through the French Embassy he also obtained permission from the Home Office to visit English prisons and he made extensive studies of Newgate, Millbank and Pentonville. Apparently he intended to write about them at some length, but the project did not materialize.

His exhibit continued to pay handsome dividends. Before he left England he sold three of his paintings, all by William van de Velde, and realized a profit of more than six hundred pounds. His sojourn in England had been profitable as well as pleasant.

By early May, 1846, Vidocq was reunited with his wife at Saint-Mandé, and together they pondered the problem of whether to close the Information Bureau or make a concerted effort to expand its operations. Fleuride wanted her seventy-one-year-old husband to retire, but he insisted he had too much energy. "There is much I have yet to accomplish," he told Dumas.

On May 9, 1846, a Paris newspaper, the *Democratic paci-fique,* made the mistake of announcing that Vidocq had died in poverty near Brussels after drinking to excess. The indignant old man promptly sent a letter to the publisher, Victor Considérant, who was an old friend:

> I have just read in your paper of Monday evening last, that Vidocq, the celebrated thief-taker, died lately near Brussels in a state of poverty.
>
> I trust you will be kind enough to contradict such a false statement, *as I am neither dead nor poor.* I am quite as well as I was when you honored me with your visit . . . about a year ago. As to the state of my fortune, I have more than enough for me; and if you will favor me with your company at dinner, any day you may wish to appoint, you will see a man who, for a long time yet, means to disappoint those who, for particular reasons, may wish to bid him farewell, but who has saved enough to treat his friends well.

Suddenly, in July, 1846, Vidocq made yet another trip to London. A manufacturing firm indicated an interest in leasing his paper and ink patents, and he went off to close the deal. This he accomplished during a stay of two to three weeks and returned home early in August.

This brief trip was memorable for unexpected reasons. Prince Louis Napoleon Bonaparte, nephew of the Emperor and titular head of the party of those who wanted to place him on the throne, escaped in May from the fortress prison in which King Louis Philippe had incarcerated him. He managed to reach England disguised as a laborer, then took quarters at the Brunswick Hotel in London under an assumed name.

Vidocq not only stayed at the same hotel in Jermyn Street but made it his business to call on the Prince. His attitude is curious because he had never before shown any real interest in politics. Louis Napoleon, who would return to France after the ouster of Louis-Philippe in the Revolution of 1848, win an election to the position of President of the Republic and then, in a coup, establish himself on the throne as Napoleon III, made no secret of his ambitions.

Vidocq was reported to have spent at least two hours in conversation with the Prince, but nothing else is known about their meeting. Later it was rumored that Vidocq agreed to work for the restoration of the Bonaparte dynasty, but no shred of evidence can be found to indicate whether this story is true or false. All that can be said with certainty is that the meeting took place.

There can be little doubt, either, that Vidocq, like all thinking Frenchmen, realized that another change was in the wind. Louis-Philippe was proving himself as autocratic, heavy-handed and reactionary as the Bourbons had been for centuries. The middle class had turned against him, and many felt, with the workers and artisans, that the time was ripe for the establishment of a republic. The Bonapartists were still conspiring to overthrow the regime, and even members of the old aristocracy were lukewarm in their support for the monarch who had broken his promises to every class.

So it may be that Vidocq, for the first time, was playing the game of politics for the sake of his own future. Be that as it may, in the autumn of 1846, he had more than enough personal problems to keep him occupied.

XVII

IN THE AUTUMN OF 1846 Fleuride Vidocq was stricken with cancer, and the disease made such rapid progress that she was soon confined to her bed. She needed heavy doses of laudanum and other opiates to ease her pain and became a helpless invalid before the end of the year. Her husband gave up all activities, staying at Saint-Mandé to remain at her side and, for all practical purposes, turned over the Information Bureau to his junior associates.

He received offers of as much as 25,000 francs from prospective buyers of the detective agency, but refused to even consider them. The Information Bureau was his own creation, and he had no intention of allowing others to trade on his reputation and achievements.

His finances deteriorated while he nursed his wife. French bankers, merchants and other men of substance were sending large sums of money abroad for safekeeping as it became increasingly apparent that King Louis-Philippe would not survive the gathering storm. The value of bonds and property declined drastically, and in the worsening economic recession many hitherto solvent people became bankrupt.

Among them were men to whom Vidocq had loaned money, and it was impossible for him to recoup. Had he been in Paris there might have been some way to slow the drain and protect his various investments, but he shrugged off his losses. The solace he could offer his wife was more important to him than money.

Fleuride Vidocq died on September 22, 1847, after an illness of a year and was buried in the churchyard at Saint-Mandé. Even though her death had been anticipated, her loss was a great shock.

Several weeks later when Vidocq began to recover his equilibrium, he began to realize that his affairs were in a shambles. The Information Bureau had lost most of its clients, so he closed its doors permanently and, at the same time, sold the little estate at Saint-Mandé. He moved into Paris, renting a small house at 31, rue Saint-Louis, filling it to overflowing with his best furniture, bric-a-brac and paintings from his country house and the offices in the Galerie Vivienne. At the age of seventy-two he was starting a new life.

It was his intention to live in retirement, emerging from it occasionally to act as a private detective on behalf of friends whose cases interested him. He planned to dine at the better restaurants with members of the literary and legal professions, as he had been doing for so many years. He would take daily strolls and dawdle away a few hours in sidewalk cafés. Naturally, he would also maintain his liaisons with various young women of the theater and, undoubtedly, would become involved in new romances, too.

Even though his finances were somewhat depleted, he had more than enough money for his needs. He hired a woman to act as his housekeeper, assuring her that her duties would be light. All she would need to do would be to keep his apartment clean and attend to his laundry. He ate very little for breakfast and expected to have few of his other meals at home.

The prospect appealed to a man of seventy-two who had worked hard all of his life. All that disturbed him was that he would move out of the limelight, but he appeared to feel certain that the occasional cases he would take as a detective would create new publicity.

Less than six months later Vidocq's situation changed overnight.

On February 22, 1848, the people of Paris erected barricades for the first time in eighteen years, and the next day troops made the grave error of firing into a crowd of demonstrators. The Revolution of 1848 was in full sway, and on February 24, the tired, bewildered Louis-Philippe abdicated and fled to England where he died three years later.

The liberals grasped their chance and, meeting at the Hôtel de Ville, established the Second Republic. Alphonse de Lamartine, the poet-diplomat-soldier, became provisional President, and Landrin, who had been Vidocq's attorney, moved into the second highest place at the Ministry of Justice as Procurator General.

Everyone in and out of positions of authority wanted to keep watch on everyone else. There were factions within the ranks of the republicans; the Bourbons wanted to place Louis-Philippe's grandson on the throne; and the Bonapartists were clamoring for the return of Louis Napoleon. The manpower of the Brigade de la Sûreté, still commanded by Allard, was almost doubled, and a new organization, the Sûreté Générale, which included the provincial offices of the original Sûreté and had a large Paris office as well, was formed under a man named Carteret.

Vidocq, who was approaching his seventy-third birthday, was recruited by Lamartine and Landrin to serve in the new Sûreté Générale. He responded with the enthusiasm of a man fifty years younger, donning various disguises and reporting on the plots and counterplots that were keeping politicians of all persuasions busy. Virtually nothing specific is known about his activities until the time of the June insurrection, when the working classes went into the streets again to demonstrate their dissatisfaction with the new government.

Although Vidocq was too old to mingle with street mobs, there were valuable functions he could perform, and Lamartine sent him to London to learn the intentions of Prince

Louis Napoleon. The old master detective arrived in England early in July, and went straight to the source by dining with the ambitious head of the Bonaparte faction.

Again, no details of their conference are known. Nothing was committed to paper, and Vidocq made no mention of the meeting in any letters. It can be gleaned from his subsequent attitudes, however, that he threw in his lot with the Bonapartists and thereafter was a fervent supporter of the Prince.

Vidocq continued to work for the Sûreté after his return to Paris in August and seems to have continued to conduct political rather than criminal surveillances, as this was the new bureau's function. He attended meetings of various factions in disguise, then sent in cryptic reports to his superiors, but his usefulness was rapidly coming to an end.

Late in the autumn a new constitution was adopted, and in December an election was held with the voters overwhelmingly expressing themselves in favor of Louis Napoleon. The new President came to Paris in triumph, and no one cheered him more loudly than Vidocq.

At the end of February, 1849, Vidocq performed his last major task. Various enemies of the new Bonaparte government were imprisoned in the Conciergerie where they were believed to be plotting against the administration. So Vidocq ended his career as he had started it, and acted as a police spy.

He was imprisoned in the Conciergerie on hazy charges and spent two months in jail, being released in April with no mention of either his eight-week term or its conclusion being recorded at the prison. Presumably he mingled with the plotters and passed along word of their machinations to the Sûreté Générale.

The time had come for him to retire, and he could have lived on an annuity of almost 4000 francs per year. He also badgered the new government into paying him a pension of 1200 francs per year and he had other income from investments that had not soured.

His first act was an attempt to have his pension increased, and he wrote to the government, claiming he was destitute. An inspector paid him a visit, and the old actor rose to the occasion, giving one of his most stirring performances.

He wore his oldest, shabbiest clothes, aided by makeup that made him appear gaunt. It was true, he admitted, that the apartment had nine rooms and was filled with expensive furnishings. But it wasn't his apartment. He occupied one small bedroom, which the friends who rented the place allowed him to use as an act of charity. He tried to pay his fair share for the food he consumed, but he had so little money that he had to rely on the kindness of his friends to prevent starvation. His seedy clothes spoke for themselves. In brief, he was a pitiful old man.

The inspector was deeply touched, and further investigation proved that the apartment was not rented in Vidocq's name. All the facts seemed to tally.

The government didn't want to be shamed, and the wily Vidocq's pension was promptly increased by 1000 francs per year. He had won his final battle with the bureaucrats, much to his delight.

The incident was responsible for the story that he spent his last years in poverty, and this supposed fact was confirmed by the newspaper obituaries written at the time of his death. The claim was anything but true, however, and Vidocq lived in solid comfort during his final years.

His house had nine crowded rooms, which were cleaned by his one servant, a middle-aged woman with whom he quarreled incessantly. His letters to Ledru and other friends were filled with complaints about this "sour termagant." He still dined one or two nights each week with old friends, but his social life was less active than it had been for many years, and he did not hesitate to bombard long-time associates with notes telling them that he was lonely.

Vidocq still maintained his relations with accessible young women, so his loneliness was only relative. Because of his somewhat diminished financial circumstances he could no longer give them expensive gifts, but his ingenuity was equal to the test.

He brought his various mistresses home with him and let them enjoy his expensive furniture, his collection of paintings, his exquisite bric-a-brac. Then he told each in turn that he would make her the sole beneficiary of his will. No sooner said than done: he wrote a new will, and the greedy woman was happy to go on with the affair.

What none of his many mistresses knew was that Vidocq took care to ensure that none of these last testaments were legally binding. Under French law it was necessary for the signing of a will to be witnessed by three persons, but not one of these documents was witnessed by anyone.

After he died in 1857 at the age of eighty-two, no fewer than eleven women claimed his estate, each of them brandishing a will. The courts declared all of these documents invalid.

At some time during his last years Vidocq was visited by a man who called himself Emile-Adolph Vidocq and who claimed to be his son. His mother was Louise Chevalier, Vidocq's unfaithful first wife, and his real father was an Arras attorney named Leduc. Emile-Adolph offered a deal: in return for an immediate cash settlement he would abandon all claims to the estate of the man whose surname he had appropriated.

Vidocq not only threw him out of the house, but wrote a long, detailed codicil to his real will, in which he explained why it would have been impossible for him to have sired Emile-Adolph. These precautions paid off. Emile-Adolph was one of the claimants to his estate, but the courts ruled that he could not have been Vidocq's son, and he was compelled to drop his suit.

In his last years Vidocq continued to yearn for a more active life and bombarded the Ministry of Justice, Ministry of the Interior and even the Prefect of Paris police for work. These pathetic requests were ignored.

Occasionally a private client still hired him, however, and until he was eighty Vidocq remained active, tracking down swindlers and confidence men. In the last case on which he is known to have worked, he traced the missing funds of a large company to a female bookkeeper who was using the money to support a lover.

Late in 1852 President Bonaparte seized the throne in a coup and reestablished the Empire, calling himself Napoleon III. No one was more pleased than the seventy-seven-year-old Vidocq, who daydreamed that he would be made head of the Sûreté. But his letters to the Emperor and various ministers were ignored, and he was hurt, unable to realize that his active career was ended.

But Vidocq still had the power to intrigue posterity. In 1853 he formed a friendship with the proprietor of an upholstery shop and his wife, Alexis and Anne-Héloïse Lefèvre. Soon he made an arrangement to eat all his meals at their house.

Before and after his death old friends speculated in vain on his relationship with Anne-Héloïse. According to his last, legitimate will her maiden name had been Guillemot, and Ledru wrote that she was "a young lady of great charm." Literally nothing else is known about her, and neither Vidocq's contemporaries nor later generations have ever learned whether she was his mistress or not.

In 1855, when he was eighty, Vidocq moved for the last time, renting a spacious eight-room apartment at 2, rue Saint-Pierre-Popincourt, only a short distance from his previous residence. The Lefèvres occupied these quarters with him, and it was their joint home. Presumably on those occasions when he entertained actresses and other light ladies, as he sometimes did, Alexis and Anne-Héloïse discreetly withdrew.

The decline in Vidocq's standing during his last years was a process of natural attrition. Younger, more active men were at the country's helm, and younger, more active criminals were being tracked by younger, more active detectives and policemen. Only Vidocq himself failed to realize that he had made his contribution and that he was no longer needed. Some of his friends, like Balzac, were dead; others, Hugo among them, had gone into exile to protest the despotism of Napoleon III; still others, like Ledru, were in retirement.

But Vidocq never stopped scheming, never stopped planning, never gave up the hope that he would return to active service. The Sûreté Nationale, its various elements finally combined into a permanent, unified force under Napoleon III, had forgotten his existence, and not until after his death would his contributions to society be recalled and appreciated.

In his last years few people recognized the old man, impeccably dressed, diamond cuff links and shirtstuds flashing, who strolled with the aid of a gold-handled walking stick. But he still had an eye for an attractive woman, and sometimes was still successful; three of the young women who presented spurious wills after his death had affairs with him during the last two years of his life.

Late in 1854 Vidocq suffered an attack of cholera, but Anne-Héloïse nursed him back to health and, astonishingly, he made a complete recovery. The following year, when he was eighty, he sent a long letter to Napoleon III in which he made specific suggestions for the reorganization of the Sûreté. The communication went unanswered, and his ideas were ignored until 1878, when a permanent crime detection laboratory was established, with chemists and ballistics experts on the permanent payroll.

In 1855, too, Vidocq made another attempt to have his pension increased and bombarded the authorities with letters. Either they were weary of reading letters from him, had forgotten what he had done or had decided his pension was adequate. Whatever their reasons, they did not bother to reply.

On April 30, 1857, Vidocq ate a large dinner with the Lefèvres and drank the better part of a bottle of wine. He retired to the sitting room, as was his custom, and a maidservant brought him a glass of port. As he raised it to his lips it dropped to the floor, and he discovered that his left side was paralyzed.

The stroke sent him to bed, but his mind remained unimpaired, and he lingered for the better part of two weeks. He dictated a legitimate last will and testament to the faithful Ledru, which included instructions for his funeral and the alms he wanted distributed. He left his entire estate to Anne-Héloïse Lefèvre, who would inherit almost 10,000 francs in cash, furniture and the collection of paintings. He requested burial in the churchyard of Saint-Mandé beside his wife.

On May 10 Vidocq received the last rites of the Church and the following day at dawn he died, lucid to the end, with Anne-Héloïse beside him. In another month and a half he would have been eighty-two years old.

Even before his body was removed the Paris police, who had long memories, came to the apartment and confiscated what remained of his records and files.

Vidocq's funeral was held on May 12 in the Church of Saint-Denis on the rue Saint-Louis. Anne-Héloïse and Alexis Lefèvre were the chief mourners, and about two hundred persons attended, among them a group of nuns from a nearby convent to whom Vidocq had been making quiet contributions for at least ten years.

Charles Ledru, among others, observed that "an exceptionally handsome young woman" sat alone in a rear pew and wept copiously throughout the funeral service.

An Apology

I FEEL COMPELLED to apologize to the reader who, wanting to learn more about Vidocq's life and exploits, consults the brief bibliography that follows this note. Alas, the pickings are slim, and these works borrow freely from each other.

In a sense, however, it is fitting that an air of mystery continues to surround Vidocq a century and a half after his own time, and that there are still blanks in his story. He would have enjoyed posterity's inability to sift fiction from fact during his early years of adventure, and he would have been delighted by the inability of latter-day literary detectives to learn more about the lovely and elusive Annette.

It may be that the unexplained details are of no consequence. I am inclined to suspect that the wily Vidocq, enjoying himself thoroughly, deliberately veiled portions of his life story that he didn't want revealed.

As he himself noted so frequently, his accomplishments do speak for themselves.

Samuel Edwards

A Selected Bibliography

Anonymous. *Vie et Aventures de Vidocq.* Paris, 1830.

Anonymous. *Histoire Complète de Vidocq.* Paris, 1842; revised, 1843.

Anonymous. *Histoire Complète de F.-E. Vidocq.* Paris, 1858.

Edwards, Samuel. *Victor Hugo.* New York, 1971.

Froment, A. *Histoire de Vidocq.* Paris, 1829.

G———. *Histoire de Vidocq.* Paris, 1829.

Gerson, Noel B. *The Prodigal Genius: A Biography of Honoré de Balzac.* New York, 1972.

Hamre, L. *Vidocq, Maître du Crime.* Paris, 1930.

Hodgetts, E. A. B. *Vidocq: A Master of Crime.* London, 1929.

Ledru, Charles. *La Vie de Vidocq.* Paris, 1857.

———. *Mémoires.* Paris, 1860.

Maurice, Barthélemy. *Vidocq.* Paris, 1858.

Savant, Jean. *La Vie Fabuleuse et Authentique de Vidocq.* Paris, 1950.

Stead, Philip J. *Vidocq: A Biography.* London, 1953.

Vidocq, F.-E. *Mémoires.* Paris, 1828–1829; London, 1829–1830.

———. *Le Paravoleur.* Paris, 1830.

———. *Les Voleurs.* Paris, 1836.

———. *Les Vrais Mystères de Paris.* Paris, 1844.

———. *Les Chauffeurs du Nord.* Paris, 1845–1846.